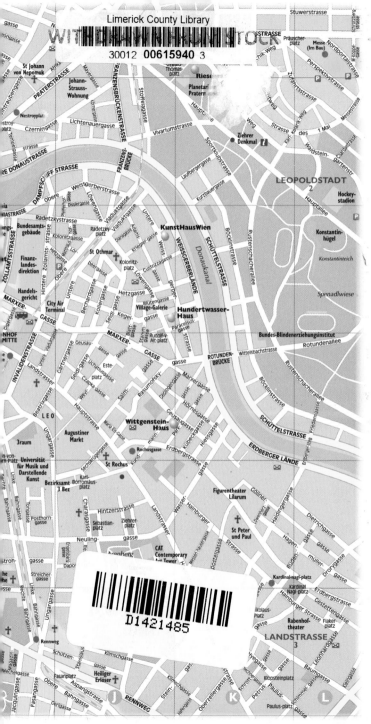

CITYPACK TOP 25
Vienna

LOUIS JAMES

If you have any comments
or suggestions for this guide
you can contact the editor at
Citypack@theAA.com

AA Publishing
Find out more about AA Publishing and the wide
range of services the AA provides by visiting our
website at www.theAA.com/travel

How to Use This Book

KEY TO SYMBOLS

✚ Map reference to the accompanying fold-out map

✉ Address

☎ Telephone number

🕐 Opening/closing times

🍴 Restaurant or café

🚆 Nearest rail station

Ⓜ Nearest subway (Metro) station

🚌 Nearest bus route

🚢 Nearest riverboat or ferry stop

♿ Facilities for visitors with disabilities

❓ Other practical information

▷ Further information

ℹ Tourist information

✋ Admission charges: Expensive (over €10), Moderate (€5–€10), and Inexpensive (€5 or less)

⭐ Major Sight   ★ Minor Sight

👣 Walks   🚐 Excursions

🛍 Shops

🎷 Entertainment and Nightlife

🍴 Restaurants

This guide is divided into four sections

• Essential Vienna: An introduction to the city and tips on making the most of your stay.
• Vienna by Area: We've broken the city into five areas, and recommended the best sights, shops, entertainment venues, nightlife and restaurants in each one. Suggested walks help you to explore on foot.
• Where to Stay: The best hotels, whether you're looking for luxury, budget or something in between.
• Need to Know: The info you need to make your trip run smoothly, including getting about by public transport, weather tips, emergency phone numbers and useful websites.

Navigation In the Vienna by Area chapter, we've given each area its own colour, which is also used on the locator maps throughout the book and the map on the inside front cover.

Maps The fold-out map accompanying this book is a comprehensive street plan of Vienna. The grid on this fold-out map is the same as the grid on the locator maps within the book. We've given grid references within the book for each sight and listing.

Contents

CONTENTS

Introducing Vienna

Set in the heart of Central Europe, Vienna has always attracted visitors for its imperial treasures and outstanding cultural heritage. However it has also begun to gain a reputation for being trendy and funky.

The Rathausplatz has become particularly lively. People gather here for ice skating in winter, for the Social Democrats' 1 May parade and for the spectacular opening of the Vienna Arts Festival shortly afterward. There are open-air showings of music and opera films every evening in July and August, and from mid-November to Christmas Eve the glittering *Christkindlmarkt* is a major family attraction. It is also from here that the *Silvesterpfad* (New Year's Eve Walk) starts its meandering route toward Stephansplatz, where the Cathedral's great bell rings in the New Year while the crowds dance to the Blue Danube Waltz.

The Hofburg is another focal point of the city. In the Imperial Treasury you come face to face with the history of Central Europe, Habsburg power and the symbolic relics of Empire; if treasures are not your bag, you can see a musical performance of the Spanish Riding School; or if you're prepared to rise early on a Sunday, go along to a sung mass performed by the Vienna Boys' Choir in the Burgkapelle. But the 'Burg' is not only a monument to the past; history is still being made here. Politicians, diplomats, officials and scientists from all over the world have been assembling in the Hofburg since Vienna became the third official seat of the United Nations.

The cosmopolitan metropolis of Vienna is not typical of Austria as a whole. It is rather an icon of the rich past of Central Europe; but at the same time it is ultramodern, a new economic hot spot, as its businesses take advantage of the fall of the Iron Curtain and seize new opportunities for investment.

Facts + Figures

- **The population of Vienna is 1.7 million. The non-Austrian population of Vienna stands at more than 19 per cent.**
- **Of the 185,000 Jewish-Viennese who lived here before World War II, 50,000 died in the Holocaust.**

VIENNESE DIALECT

Viennese dialect is sophisticated and has a long tradition on stage and in cabaret, even in verse. Vivid, but impenetrable to outsiders, it is both a vibrant assertion of identity and a means whereby the Viennese can shelter their own private sphere in a city full of tourists and new arrivals.

LOCAL CONSERVATISM

The Viennese exhibit strong local patriotism, coupled with a conservatism that ensures each new architectural project is greeted with cries of scorn. It was ever so: The critics complained of the opera on its completion in 1869 that it looked like an 'elephant lying down to digest its dinner'.

MUST BE TIME FOR A MEAL

An astonishing 4,000 eateries cater to the Viennese need for meals at all times of day. Extracurricular consumption includes at least one 'coffee-pause' in the morning, and maybe a *Jause* (a hefty snack of bread, charcuterie and cheese) to stave off hunger pangs between serious eating. The locals cheerfully joke about 'suicide by knife and fork', being no more perturbed by this prospect than their forefathers were by the abuse of medieval moralists (and the poet Schiller), who compared them to the Phaeacians, a gluttonous and pleasure-loving people in Homer's *Odyssey*.

A Short Stay in Vienna

DAY 1

Morning Start at the Opera (U-Bahn and tram stops). Just behind it is the famous **Hotel Sacher** (▷ 112) where you can enjoy a coffee and a slice of Sachertorte in the hotel's coffeehouse. Proceed to the nearby **Kapuzinergruft** (Imperial Crypt, ▷ 29) on the Neuer Markt to view the tombs of the Habsburg emperors.

Mid-morning Adjacent to the Neuer Markt is Kärntner Strasse, from which you approach **Stephansdom** (St. Stephen's Cathedral, ▷ 31), the spiritual and topographical heart of the city. From the deeply sacred, move abruptly to the very secular: in a narrow backstreet behind the cathedral is the **Mozarthaus** (▷ 34) where the composer wrote his most satirical work, *The Marriage of Figaro*.

Lunch Enjoy a meal in the intimate garden of the **Haas & Haas** teahouse (▷ 39), accessed from the southwest corner of the cathedral square (Stephansplatz).

Afternoon From Stephansplatz walk north along the Graben, then turn left down the Kohlmarkt. Ahead of you is the vast complex of the **Hofburg** (▷ 26), the former Imperial Palace of the Habsburgs. Cross the Ringstrasse via the Heldentor to the **Kunsthistorisches Museum** (▷ 52) with its superb collection of pictures and applied art.

Dinner Across the River Wien a fine-dining experience awaits you at **Steirereck** (▷ 89), arguably Vienna's finest restaurant.

Evening Close the day with a trip along the Ringstrasse on Tram 1 to view the great Historicist architecture of the 19th century, beautifully illuminated at night.

Morning Start the day with breakfast in **Café Schwarzenberg** (▷ 62) opposite the **Hotel Imperial** (▷ 112) on the Ringstrasse. From there it is a short walk to the **Hochstrahlbrunnen** (▷ 85), a 19th-century fountain, and the less impressive but huge Russian War Memorial behind it, both at the southern end of Schwarzenbergplatz. Then bear left and follow the Rennweg to the main entrance of **Schloss Belvedere** (▷ 82).

Mid-morning The highlight of the Lower Belvedere is the Golden Salon (*cabinet doré*) and Balthasar Permoser's statue (1721) of Prince Eugene of Savoy, whose palace this was. Climb the hill through the park to the Upper Belvedere with its splendid collection of paintings, including works by Klimt, Schiele and Kokoschka.

Lunch Try the traditional Viennese dish of *Tafelspitz* (boiled beef) at the nearby restaurant **Sperl** (▷ 89) and finish off with a *Powidltascherln*—the word may seem unpronounceable, but the sweet dumplings with plum compôte are irresistible.

Afternoon For a complete change of theme and scene, take Tram O from Südbahnhof to Praterstern. In the **Prater** (▷ 97) you can take a ride on the Ferris Wheel or one of the many other attractions before going back to Schwedenplatz with U1 (U-Bahn). From here it is a short walk to the **Jewish Quarter** (▷ 28) and Judenplatz.

Dinner Indulge in some people-watching in the glassed terrace of Vienna's top Italian restaurant, **Fabios** (▷ 43).

Evening Take in an opera performance in the **Staatsoper** (▷ 35) or a concert in the gilded auditorium of the **Musikverein** (▷ 88).

Top 25 ^{TOP}25

ESSENTIAL VIENNA TOP 25

8

These pages are a quick guide to the Top 25, which are described in more detail later. Here they are listed alphabetically, and the tinted background shows which area they are in.

Danube Cruise ▷ 94 Cruises within Vienna and downstream to the Slovak capital, Bratislava.

Freud Museum ▷ 68 For 47 years the home of the founder of psychoanalysis until his emigration in 1938.

Freyung ▷ 25 Baroque palaces and the monastery which gave the square its name.

Heeresgeschichtliches Museum ▷ 80 A military-history museum in a vast complex.

Hofburg ▷ 26–27 The former Imperial Palace was the Habsburg dynasty's residence for six centuries.

Hundertwasser-Haus and KunstHausWien ▷ 95 Postmodern follies designed by Friedensreich Hundertwasser.

Jewish Quarter ▷ 28 One of Vienna's oldest and most historic quarters, centred on Judenplatz.

Kahlenburg ▷ 96 A spur of the Wienerwald with fine views over the city.

Kapuzinergruft ▷ 29 Richly ornate coffins in the Imperial Crypt.

Karlskirche ▷ 81 St. Charles's Church is a masterwork of Fischer von Erlach, father and son.

Museum für Angewandte Kunst ▷ 30 Vienna's Museum of Applied Art.

Liechtenstein Museum ▷ 69 A palace housing the Liechtenstein family's art collection.

Kunsthistorisches Museum ▷ 52–53 Famous works by Bruegel and Rubens.

◀ ◀ ◀

Shopping

There are always limits to how much a visitor can integrate into a local style and these are reached quite quickly with *Tracht* (traditional costume), found in shops all over the city. But you do not need to go the whole hog of *Dirndlkleid* or *Lederhosen*: The more restrained *Steirer-Jacke* (Styrian jacket with decorative edgings) or the wonderfully enduring Loden overcoats, or even a smart Austrian hat can still look good when you get home.

Souvenirs and Gifts

Austrians are good at designing charming ornaments, some admittedly bordering on kitsch. Typical are the models of animals and birds made in a variety of different materials. Decorative enamel influenced by the Wiener Werkstätte, the leading producer of which is Michaela Frey, is also attractive, while ladies' purses and handbags embroidered with petit point also make nice presents. Porcelain comes from two great names: Augarten in Vienna and the Gmundner Keramik from Upper Austria. The latter, with its wavy green motifs, is vernacular, while the Augarten is formal and aristocratic.

Local Delicacies

Vienna has plenty of local delicacies. The famous Sachertorte (a chocolate cake invented in 1832) can be shipped anywhere for you from the Sacher shop, likewise the rival

SHOPPING AREAS

Vienna shopping can roughly be divided into luxury, middle market and cheap. The three sides of the rectangle comprising Kohlmarkt, Graben and Kärntner Strasse offer chic Austrian goods and international designer labels. Mariahilfer Strasse is Vienna's Oxford Street, with the last of the big stores (good for household and clothing). Cheapest of all is the flea-market (*Flohmarkt*) at the west end of the Naschmarkt each Saturday morning. Lots of bargains!

Christmas shopping; antiques-hunting; Christmas market; clothes boutique; shopping mall (top to bottom, left to right)

Imperialtorte. Then there are the Mozart Kugel (gold-wrapped spherical chocolates filled with marzipan and nougat) and the Mozart Thaler (the same, but shaped like coins). These are the trademark Austrian chocolates, but many other chocolatiers produce chocolates just as good. Austrian wine remains much underrated (the whites, such as Grüner Veltliner or Riesling from the Wachau, are recommended) and the *Sekt* is better than its reputation as the poor man's champagne. *Obstler* (schnapps made from various fruits) is an Austrian specialty much prized by connoisseurs.

Traditional Music

Nothing gives a better taste of a country than its music. Naturally a huge selection of CDs of Austrian music (including one-off performances such as the New Year's Concert of the Vienna Philharmonic at the Musikverein) is on sale in the city. Works by Johann Strauss (the 'Waltz King') are ubiquitous, as are the indigenous art form of operetta (Lehár, Kálmán) and 'Schrammel music' from the *Heurigen* (taverns). Austrian Broadcasting (ORF) has produced a comprehensive anthology of *Wiener Lieder*, featuring singers like Walter Berry and Angelika Kirchschlager. A fascinating collector's item is the ORF CD of the music of ethnic minorities in Austria, '*Hausgemacht*'. Music to accompany performances of the Spanish Riding School can be obtained on CD.

SHOPPING CULTURE HAS CHANGED

Time was when Viennese shopkeepers called all the shots, but much has changed. Despite a long rearguard action by retailers, shopping hours have been greatly liberalized: No longer do sad crowds mill around the windows of closed shops on Saturday afternoon; no more do bookstore assistants crouch over the tills, glaring suspiciously at browsers. And for those who want to shop till they drop, there are now several constantly expanding shopping malls. The biggest is the aptly named Shopping City Süd. An alternative is the Ringstrassen Galerien.

Shopping by Theme

Whether you're looking for a department store, a quirky boutique, or something in between, you'll find it all in Vienna. On this page shops are listed by theme. For a more detailed write-up, see the individual listings in Vienna by Area.

Vienna by Night

New *Szenelokale* (trendy or 'in' bars and restaurants) open every year in Vienna. These are concentrated in certain areas—the best known is the so-called *Bermuda Dreieck* (Bermuda Triangle) to the west of Schwedenplatz.

Where to Go
Less self-consciously chic and utterly charming is the Spittelberg area, a good example of inner-city revival. Here you can sit in an 18th-century courtyard, or on a street flanked by baroque and Biedermeier façades, enjoying Austrian regional or ethnic cooking, or check out the many bars and Italian-style cafés. A fun night-time atmosphere has developed in the area from Stephansdom to Am Hof and between Josefstädterstrasse and Laudongasse in the Josefstadt, a region frequented by intellectuals and the well-to-do.

Wine Taverns
An entire culture revolves around the wine-taverns of Vienna's peripheral villages, Grinzing, Heiligenstadt, Salmannsdorf and Neustift am Walde being the best known. You may prefer this to the bustle of the city; here you can sip white wine in the peace of a *Heuriger* (▷ 106) garden and tuck into a *Heuriger* pork roast.

Floodlit Monuments
Perhaps the greatest evening pleasure is entirely free, namely walking around the floodlit monuments of the Inner City.

Rathaus at dusk; sunset on the Danube; Karlskirche illuminated at night (top to bottom)

BALMY EVENINGS
Exploiting five and a half months of mild to warm weather, in Vienna you can linger at café or restaurant tables on the pavement outside, or in *Heurigen* gardens, until late into the evening. A restaurant extension is known as a *Schanigarten* from the nickname of the first person to erect one on the Graben in 1754. In summer there are also major open-air events: among them the jazz festival on the Donau-Insel and the opera films in front of the Rathaus.

Eating Out

The general standard of Viennese cuisine is high, even at the cheaper end of the market. The Nordsee chain offers very acceptable fast food fish dishes and there is a broad range of middle-price *gute bürgerliche Küche* (good bourgeois cuisine). But gourmets will not go hungry either.

Ethnic Influences

Vienna's kitchen has always been a mixture of Austrian recipes and those of its Central European neighbours, formerly part of the Habsburg Empire. The famous *Wiener Schnitzel* is derived from the *scaloppina Milanese* from Lombardy, goulash was imported from Hungary, and some Bohemian dishes (chiefly various kinds of dumplings) have survived here, even when they are now hard to find in the Czech lands. Over the past decade, an invasion of Turkish doner kebab has followed the pizza wave, although this is more a feature of the suburbs than the main tourist areas.

Run the Gamut from Beef to Ice Cream

Austria is a land-locked country and Vienna's cooking has always focused on meat and cereals. Beef (especially boiled beef called *Tafelspitz*) has a long tradition in the city and in a few restaurants that concentrate on it, the variety of beef dishes is amazing. Everything depends upon the quality of the beef itself, as well as careful preparation and fresh condiments if the real *Tafelspitz* experience is to be enjoyed. Moving from the savoury to the sweet, Vienna's ice-cream salons have a selection and quality to rival those of Italy.

THAT UNIQUE LOCAL EXPERIENCE

Specific to Vienna are the *Heurigen* (wine taverns) on the outskirts of the city. In the old town of the inner city, there are also deep wine cellars sometimes descending two levels through baroque to Gothic foundations. Above ground in summer, you can lunch in one of the popular garden restaurants or dine in a princely palace.

Viennese cakes and pastries—especially the famous Sachertorte—can be enoyed in the city's coffeehouses

Restaurants by Cuisine

There are restaurants to suit all tastes and budgets in Vienna. On this page they are listed by cuisine. For a more detailed description of each restaurant, see Vienna by Area.

ASIAN

Akakiko (▷ 62)
Green Cottage (▷ 62)
Safran (▷ 75)

BEISL

Beim Czaak (▷ 43)
Glacisbeisl (panel, ▷ 54)
Kern's Beisel (▷ 44)

CELLARS

Augustinerkeller (▷ 43)
Esterhazykeller (▷ 43)
Piaristenkeller (▷ 63)
Rathauskeller (▷ 63)
Salm Bräu (▷ 89)
Zwölf-Apostelkeller
   (▷ 45)

COFFEEHOUSES AND CAFÉS

Aida (▷ 43)
Berg (▷ 75)
Café Landmann (▷ 62)
Café Schwarzenberg
   (▷ 62)
Demel (▷ 43)
Diglas (▷ 43)
Dommayer (▷ 106)
Heiner (▷ 44)
Prückel (▷ 45)
Rebhuhn (▷ 75)

Tirolerhof (▷ 45)
Trzesniewski (▷ 45)

HEURIGEN

Alter Bach-Hengl (▷ 106)
Fuhrgassl-Huber (▷ 106)
Mayer am Pfarrplatz
   (▷ 106)
Zimmerman (▷ 106)

INTERNATIONAL

Bodega Española (▷ 89)
Couscous (▷ 75)
Do & Do (▷ 43)
Ilona-Stüberl (▷ 44)

ITALIAN

Casa Alberto (▷ 89)
Da Bizi (▷ 43)
Fabios (▷ 43)
Novelli Bacaro con Cucina
   (▷ 45)
Riegi (▷ 45)

SEAFOOD

Hummerbar (▷ 44)
Kornat (▷ 44)
Nordsee (▷ 45)
Ragusa (▷ 75)

VEGETARIAN

Wrenkh (▷ 45)

VIENNA'S BEST

Coburg (▷ 62)
Donauturm (▷ 106)
Himmelsstube (▷ 63)
Im Palais Schwarzenberg
   (▷ 89)
Korso bei der Oper (▷ 44)
Plachutta (▷ 106)
Sluka (▷ 63)
Steirereck im Stadtpark
   (▷ 89)

VIENNESE/AUSTRIAN

Alte Backstube (▷ 62)
Eiles (▷ 62)
Figlmüller (▷ 44)
Haas & Haas (▷ 44)
Kupferdachl (▷ 63)
Meinl am Graben (▷ 45)
Roth (▷ 75)
Servitenstüberl (▷ 75)
Smutny (▷ 63)
Sperl (▷ 89)
Zu ebener Erde und erster
   Stock (▷ 63)
Zum schwarzen Kameel
   (▷ 45)
Zur kleinen Steiermark
   (▷ 89)

If You Like...

However you'd like to spend your time in Vienna, these top suggestions should help you tailor your ideal visit. Each sight or listing has a fuller write-up in Vienna by Area.

CLASSICAL MUSIC

Practise your conducting in the Haus der Musik (▷ 33).
Savour the musicianship of the Wiener Philharmoniker in the Golden Hall of the Musikverein (▷ 88).
Pay homage to Mozart at the Mozarthaus (▷ 34).

COFFEEHOUSES

Order the original Sachertorte at Café Sacher, in Hotel Sacher (▷ 112)—or have it mailed to friends from the Sacher shop.
Meet friends at Café Landtmann (▷ 62).
Indulge yourself at Demel patisserie (▷ 43), a former purveyor to the imperial household.

Musikverein (top); cakes galore in Vienna's coffee-houses (above)

ANTIQUES SHOPPING

Buy Augarten porcelain (▷ 38) decorated with floral designs in the former Augarten Palace, now a factory for this famous ware.
Consult the experts on Secessionist art at Christian Nebehay's gallery/shop (▷ 39).
Bid at an auction at 'Aunt Dorothy' (Dorotheum, ▷ 38), Vienna's traditional auction house.

CLOTHES

Have a gentleman's suit made for you at Knize's shop (▷ 39).
Be daring with a bit of vernacular fashion at Resi Hammerer (▷ 40).
Check out the headgear at Szászi Hüte—a hat for every occasion (▷ 60).

Shop for antiques (above right) or that perfect hat (right)

*The Ankeruhr; Hotel
Imperial (below)*

WHAT'S FREE

Music films on a huge screen in front of
the Rathaus (July and August, ▷ 55).
A walk to or from the Kahlenberg
through woods and vineyards (▷ 96).
Watch the figures of the Ankeruhr move
across the clockface at noon (▷ 28).

HOTELS WITH CHARACTER

Be treated like a personal guest of Prince
Schwarzenberg in this luxurious hotel (▷ 112).
Enjoy trendy British styling in Das
Triest hotel, designed by Sir Terence
Conran (▷ 112).
Combine Viennese tradition with modern
comfort at Hotel Sacher (▷ 112).
Mingle with kings and presidents at Hotel
Imperial (▷ 112), used as official accommo-
dation for state visitors.

ATMOSPHERIC RESTAURANTS

Descend three floors into the impressive Zwölf-
Apostelkeller (▷ 45) for good wine and food.
Soak in the atmosphere of the Austro-
Hungarian monarchy in the Piaristenkeller (▷ 63).
Eat in a traditional *Beisl*, such as Beim Czaak
(▷ 43).

*Eat or drink in a Viennese
cellar or* Beisl *(above)*

NIGHTLIFE

Join an evening roof walk of
St. Stephen's Cathedral (▷ 31).
Meet Vienna's high society
at the exclusive Eden Bar
(▷ 41).
Get fired up with local and
international DJs at Flex, beside
the Danube Canal (▷ 61).

St. Stephen's Cathedral after dark (left)

Secession; riding the Ferris Wheel in Prater (below)

AUSTRIAN SECESSION AND EXPRESSIONISTS

Be sure to see the 'Golden Cabbage' on top of the Secession (▷ 56)—and the *Beethoven Frieze* in the Secession basement.

Don't miss the paintings by Klimt, Schiele and Kokoschka at the gallery in the Upper Belvedere (▷ 82).

Look inside Otto Wagner's Postsparkassen-amt (▷ 34) for its dazzling white hall.

Join a guided tour of Wagner's Kirche am Steinhof (▷ 100), which combines functionalism with beauty.

CHILDREN'S ACTIVITIES

Ride the Ferris Wheel and try some of the other attractions in the Prater (▷ 97).

Take a boat tour of the Seegrotte in Hinterbrühl (▷ 104), Europe's largest underground lake.

Get lost in the baroque labyrinth of the park at Schloss Schönbrunn (▷ 98–99).

SHOE-STRING ACCOMMODATION

Meet young people from all over the world at the Wombat's Hostels (▷ 109).

Arrive home at Pension am Operneck (▷ 109) with the arias from the opera still ringing in your ears.

Save money by staying in family-run Hotel Matauschek (▷ 109).

Even visitors on a budget will find inexpensive accommodation (above)

LUXURY LVING

Order a bottle of wine from Coburg restaurant's selection (▷ 62).

Splash out on handmade shoes by top shoemaker Ludwig Reiter (▷ 87).

Dine in the glassed terrace of Fabios, Vienna's authentic Italian eatery (▷ 43).

Splashing out on wine (right)

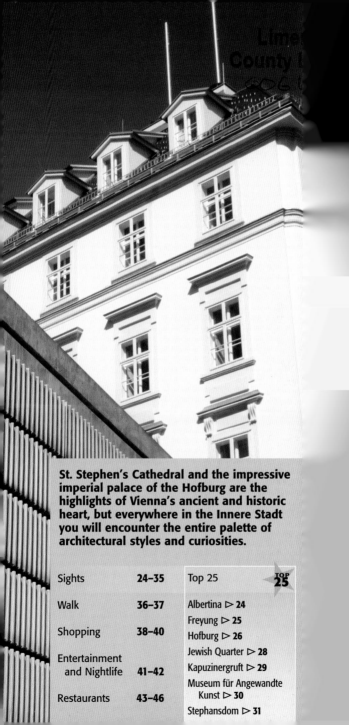

St. Stephen's Cathedral and the impressive imperial palace of the Hofburg are the highlights of Vienna's ancient and historic heart, but everywhere in the Innere Stadt you will encounter the entire palette of architectural styles and curiosities.

FRANZ-JOSEFS-KAI

Donaukanal

Börse

Börse-
platz

Rudolfs-
platz

Concordia-
platz

Salzgries

Maria am
Gestade

Schottenstift

Schottenkirche

Feuerwehr-
museum

Juden-
platz

Altes
Rathaus

Freyung

Kunstforum

Holocaust
Memorial

Jewish
Quarter

INNERE STADT

Am Hof

Uhrenmuseum

Hoher
Markt

Esperanto
Museum

Peterskirche

Minoriten-
kirche

Herrengasse

Globenmuseum

Pestsäule

Stephansdom

Minoritenplatz

Loos
Haus

Artaria
Haus

Haas-
Haus

Dom- u.
Diözesan-
museum

St
Michael

Ballhaus-
platz

Alte
Hofburg

Michaeler-
platz

Stephansplatz

Schauflergasse

Lipizzaner
Museum Wien

Stephansplatz

Schatzkammer

Stock-I-
Eisen-Platz

Sisi Museum

Hofburg

Donner
Brunnen

Neuer
Markt

Kapuzinergruft

Prinz-Eugen-
Denkmal

Nationalbibliothek

Augustiner-
kirche

Lobkowitz-
Palais

Neue
Burg

Annakirche

Burgtor
(Heldentor)

Albertina

Malteser
Kirche

Burggarten

Theatermus Gedenkr
Staatsopernmus

Albertina
Platz

Haus der
Musik

OPERNRING

Staatsoper

Stadt Theater

Walfischgasse

Mahler-
strasse

OPERNGASSE

Oper

Karlsplatz

Künstlerhaus

KÄRNTNER RING

Neuer
Markt

Karlsplatz
Pavilions

Resselpark

Karlsplatz

0   250 m

0   250 yds

SALZTOR-
BRÜCKE

FRANZ-JOSEFS-KAI

Marienbrücke

SCHWEDEN-BRÜCKE

Donaukanal

ASPERN-BRÜCKE

Ruprechtskirche

Schwedenplatz

Schwedenplatz

Urania

Fleisch-markt

Kammerspiele

Griechenbeisl

Franz-Josephs-Kai

Julius-Raab-Platz

URANIASTRASSE

Fleisch-markt

Griechenkirche

Wiesingerstrasse

Georg-Cochplatz

Regierungs-gebäude

ZOLLAMTSSTRASSE

Köllnerhof-gasse

Kammeroper

Österreichisches Postsparkassenamt

Finanzlandesdirektion

Historyworld

Jesuitenkirche

Rosenburserstrasse

STUBENRING

Bäckerstrasse

Dr-I-Seipel-Platz

Postgasse

Biberstrasse

Oskar-Kokoschka-platz

MARXER-GASSE

VORDERE

Wollzeile

Mozarthaus

Dominikanerkirche

Dominikanerbastei

Museum für Angewandte Kunst (MAK)

Schulerstrasse

Zedlitzg.

Stubenbastei

Stubentor

WEISKIRCHNER-STRASSE

BAHNHOF WIEN MITTE

Grünangergasse

Rauhensteingasse

Riemergasse

Cobdengasse

Landstrasser Hauptstrasse

Franziskanerkirche

Ballgasse

strasse

PARKRING

Schubert Denkmal

AM STADTPARK

Landstrasse Wien-mitte

Franziskaner Platz

Bruckner Denkmal

Wienfluss

Schellinggasse

gasse

gasse

Stadtpark

SCHUBERTRING

Johannesgasse

Strauss Denkmal

AM HEUMARKT

ichtegasse

ziegelg.

gasse

ÖAMTC

Kursalon

Christinengasse

Kantgasse

Lothringerstrasse

Schwarzenbergplatz

Pestalozzigasse

Beethovenplatz

Stadtpark

LOTHRINGERSTRASSE

Konzerthaus

G

H

Albertina

TOP 25

Statue of Duke Albert (left) outside the Albertina (right)

THE BASICS

www.albertina.at
🔢 F5
✉ Albertinaplatz 1
☎ 534 83-0
🕐 Daily 10–6, Wed 10–9
🍴 Restaurant and café (Do & Co, ▷ 43)
🚇 U1, U2, U4 to Karlsplatz/Oper
🚌 3A to Albertinaplatz
♿ Good
💰 Moderate
❓ Large museum shop

HIGHLIGHTS

● Dürer's *Hare*
● Dürer's *Praying Hands*
● Raffael's *Madonna of the Pomegranate*
● Rubens' *Head of a Boy*
● Collection of posters and photographs
● State Rooms

Louis Montoyer built this gallery between 1801 and 1804 to house the magnificent collection of drawings, engravings and artworks assembled by Duke Albert of Sachsen-Teschen.

Exhibits Vienna's Albertina is the world's leading graphic collection, comprising more than a million items. Its famous drawings and etchings are kept in controlled conditions to preserve them and are seldom on display, because light would damage their fragile structure. But the collection's abundance makes it possible to hold special exhibitions of the originals devoted to particular themes. Here is half a millennium of art history, beginning with items that predate Leonardo da Vinci and ending with some that are later than Andy Warhol. A small revolving show of facsimiles gives you an idea of the treasures. Since 2007, the Batliner and Forberg collections have been given to the Albertina on permanent loan, providing a high-quality survey of 20th-century art. They may be seen in a permanent exhibition from April 2008.

The building The Albertina forms the southeast end of the Hofburg complex. Its noble staircase and the brilliantly restored staterooms were built for Duke Albert of Sachsen-Teschen and his successor Archduke Charles. Originally the married quarters of Duke Albert and his wife Marie-Christine, the palace is a rare and magnificent example of Classicism and French Empire style in Vienna. In the ground floor area, the Albertina houses the Austrian Film Museum.

This irregularly shaped square acquired its name (meaning 'asylum') as a result of its association with the adjacent Benedictine monastery, which until 1848 had the right to give asylum to fugitives from justice.

Freyung Eighteenth-century paintings show a lively scene, with stall vendors, jugglers and clowns. Baroque palaces still rim the square.

Schottenkirche The Abbey Church of the 'Schotten' Benedictines, dominating the east side of the square, was called Scottish because the Latin name for Ireland was *Scotia maior*. The 15th-century Gothic altarpiece, now in the Prelacy Museum in the Schottenkirche, shows the earliest extant view of Vienna.

Palais Ferstel This structure is not actually a palace but a complex named after its architect. Inside, a glass-roofed arcade lined with gift shops leads from the Freyung to Herrengasse ('Street of the Lords'). It was formerly the seat of the Vienna Stock Exchange.

Kinsky-Palais This is one of Lukas von Hildebrandt's masterworks and was built in 1716, with a slim, elegant façade that overlooks the Freyung. Try to get a look at the ceremonial staircase inside and also its ceiling fresco, *Apotheosis of a War Hero*, which flatters Count Philipp von Daun, the military commander who first owned the palace.

THE BASICS

✚ E3

✉ Schottenkirche and Prelacy Museum: Freyung 6. Palais Ferstel: Freyung 2

☎ Schottenkirche: 534 98. Museum: 534 98 60

🕐 Schottenkirche usually 7am–9pm. Museum Thu–Sat 10–5

🍴 Café Central in Palais Ferstel

🚇 U2 to Schottentor

🚌 Hopper I

♿ Few

💰 Inexpensive

HIGHLIGHTS

Freyung
● Section of medieval cobbles in the northeast corner
● Hildebrandt's Kinsky-Palais, Freyung 4
Schottenkirche and Prelacy Museum
● Gothic wing altar, Master of the Scots 1469–80
● High altar (Ferstel)
● Tomb of Count Starhemberg
Palais Ferstel
● Danube Fountain

Hofburg

HIGHLIGHTS

● Imperial Treasury
● State Apartments with Silver Collection
● Court Chapel and Vienna Boys Choir
● Spanish Riding School
● Prunksaal of the National Library

TIP

● For a close-up view of the magnificent white horses, visit the Lipizzaner Museum in Renaissance Stallburg (▷ 34).

It is said that the Habsburgs never finished their great projects; the Hofburg (the former imperial residence), like St. Stephen's Cathedral (▷ 31) and the Habsburg Empire itself, is an example of their unfinished business.

Traditions In terms of history, the Hofburg (the Habsburg residence) is more significant than all other buildings in Vienna. It houses secular and sacred treasuries (Schatzkammer) containing the crowns of the Holy Roman Empire and of the Empire of Austria. Three institutions are still operating in the Hofburg, having survived from imperial times: the Hofmusikkapelle (Court Music Chapel) where the Wiener Sängerknaben (Vienna Boys' Choir) sing Sunday mass in the Burgkapelle (Court Chapel); the dancing horses of the Spanische

Equestrian statue of Prince Eugene of Savoy in Heroes Square; statue on the Neue Hofburg; eagle above St. Michael's Gate; imperial plate in the Sisi Museum; state apartments in the Sisi Museum (clockwise from far left)

THE BASICS

www.hofburg-wien.at
www.hofburgkapelle.at
www.srs.at

➕ E5

✉ State Apartments, Sisi Museum, Silver and Tableware Collection: Hofburg–Michaelerkuppel; Nationalbibliothek: Josefplatz 1; Burgkapelle: Hofburg–Schweizerhof

☎ State Apartments, Sisi Museum, Silver and Tableware Collection: 533 75 70; Nationalbibliothek: 534 10-0; Burgkapelle: 533 99 27

🕐 State Apartments, Sisi Museum, Silver and Tableware Collection: daily 9–5; Treasury: Wed–Mon 10–6; Burgkapelle: Mass mid-Sep to Jun Sun 9.15, reservation needed; Riding School: morning training Tue–Sat 10–12, performances Sun 11, reservation needed, summer and winter break; Prunksaal of the National Library: Tue–Sun 10–6, Thu 10–9

🚇 U3 to Herrengasse

♿ Few

🎫 Expensive

Hofreitschule (Spanish Riding School); and the Nationalbibliothek (National Library). The Federal President of Austria now has his offices in a wing of the residence.

Architecture The earliest fortress here was built in 1275 on the site that later became the Schweizerhof (Swiss Court), named after the former Swiss Guard. The Schweizerhof incorporates the Gothic Burgkapelle and the Renaissance Schweizertor (Swiss Gate). There were baroque extensions of the original Hofburg. The Neue Hofburg, partially framing the Heldenplatz (Heroes Square) was built in Historicist style and completed on the eve of World War I. On the square are the equestrian statues of Prince Eugene of Savoy (hero of the Turkish Wars) and Archduke Charles (victor of the battle of Aspern against Napoleon).

Jewish Quarter

The Ankeruhr on Hoher Markt (left); the Holocaust Memorial (right) on Judenplatz

THE BASICS

✚ F3
Stadttempel
www.jmw.at
✉ Seitenstettengasse 4
☎ 535 04 31
◉ By guided tours only
Mon, Thu 11.30, 2. Closed
public hols
🚇 U1, U4 to Schwedenplatz
🚌 Bus 3A to Hoher Markt
♿ Excellent
🎫 Inexpensive

Ruprechtskirche
www.ruprechtskirche.at
✉ Ruprechtsplatz
☎ 535 60 03
◉ Mon–Fri 10–12; Mon,
Wed 3–5; Fri 10pm–1am;
Christmas to Holy Week by
appointment only
♿ Excellent
🎫 Free

Jüdisches Museum Wien
www.jmw.at
✉ Misrachi Haus,
Judenplatz 8
☎ 535 04 31
◉ Sun–Thu 10–6, Fri 10–2
🚇 U1, U3 to Stephansplatz
🚌 Bus 3A to Hoher Markt
♿ Excellent
🎫 Inexpensive

The historic Jewish Quarter of Vienna has two focal points, the old temple in Seitenstettengasse and the new Holocaust Memorial on Judenplatz. Today's Jewish community is in the Second District (Leopoldstadt), northeast of the Danube Canal.

Stadttempel Hidden behind a simple façade, the neoclassical synagogue in Seitenstettengasse is the only place of Jewish worship that survived the Nazi pogroms in Vienna. The offices of the Jewish community and other institutions are in the building. Across the street is the tiny Ruprechtskirche, the oldest existing church in the city.

Hoher Markt and Altes Rathaus En route from Judengasse to Judenplatz you cross Hoher Markt. At its northeast corner is the famous Ankeruhr (Franz Matsch, 1913). Every hour a different figure from Austrian history revolves around the clock-face, while at noon all the figures appear in sequence. The former City Hall (Altes Rathaus) in Wipplingerstrasse is overshadowed by the mighty façade of the former Bohemian Court Chancellery across the street.

Holocaust Memorial The Judenplatz was originally the heart of the medieval ghetto. Remains of a synagogue can be seen beneath the Jewish Museum at Misrachi Haus, while the square itself is now dominated by Rachel Whiteread's controversial Holocaust Memorial (1996). Parisergasse leads to Palais Obizzi with its Clock Museum.

*Imperial tombs (left);
a macabre detail of
Karl VI's tomb in the
Capuchin Crypt (right)*

Kapuzinergruft

Deceased emperors' hearts are preserved in the Augustinian Church (▷ 32), their embalmed entrails in St. Stephen's (▷ 31) and their bodies here in the Capuchin Crypt, a shrine for pilgrims and loyalists.

The Capuchins and their church The Franciscan Capuchins came to Austria in the reign of Duke (later Emperor) Matthias (1612–19), whose wife, Empress Anna, founded their monastery in 1618. The preacher Marco d'Aviano was Vienna's most celebrated Capuchin. Famously intrepid, he went into battle with the imperial forces against the Turkish army, which was besieging Vienna in 1683. He is buried in one of the church's chapels.

Simplicity The building is in accord with the austere precepts of the Capuchins. Almost the only decoration is a 1936 fresco of St. Francis of Assisi and a cross on the façade. Inside is the Kaiserkapelle (Emperor Chapel), with wooden statues of emperors Matthias and Ferdinand II, III and IV. The Chapel of the Cross has an altar by Lukas von Hildebrandt and a very moving *pietà* (Mary embracing the dead Christ).

Habsburg resting place The first emperor and empress to be buried in the crypt were Matthias and his wife Anna. Since then 138 members of the Habsburg family have been interred here, along with Maria Theresa's governess. The simple copper coffin of Joseph II, is a reminder of its occupant's distaste for religious excess.

HIGHLIGHTS

The church
● Bronze of Marco d'Aviano
● Statues of four emperors
● Marble altar by Hildebrandt
● *Pietà*, by Peter Strudel and Matthias Steinl

The crypt
● Tomb of Charles IV
● Double tomb of Franz Stephan and Maria Theresa
● Tombs of Franz Joseph and Elisabeth
● Bust of the last emperor, Karl, and coffin of the last empress, Zita

Museum für Angewandte Kunst

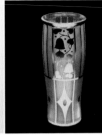

Chair (left) and graphic (middle) by Josef Hoffmann; vase by the Wiener Werkstätte (right)

THE BASICS

www.mak.at

🔲 H4

✉ Stubenring 5

☎ 711 360; recorded information 712 80 00

🕐 Tue 10–midnight, Wed–Sun 10–6. Closed 1 May, 1 Nov, 24, 25, 31 Dec

🍴 Elegant café

🚇 U3 to Stubentor

🚋 Trams 1 and 2 on Ringstrasse

🚈 Schnellbahn to Landstrasse

♿ Good

✋ Moderate

❓ Tours: audio guide. Frequent special exhibitions, often avant-garde

HIGHLIGHTS

● Atrium
● 16th-century Egyptian silk carpet
● 15th-century Buddha head
● Intarsia table from Old University (1735)
● Meissen bear
● Bohemian glass
● Lobmeyr glass (Vienna)

A striking example of minimalist display techniques at the Museum of Applied Art is the projection of silhouettes of chairs against a white screen, which emphasizes the beauty of the designs.

Forerunner Established in 1864, the MAK was the first museum of its kind in Europe. The initiative came from art historian Rudolf Eitelberger, who had been much impressed by London's South Kensington Museum, later the Victoria and Albert Museum.

Decorative The 1871 neo-Renaissance building by Heinrich Ferstel combines architecture with applied art—its façade is ornamented with sgraffito and majolica portrait medallions of artist-craftsmen.

The interior A glass-enclosed entrance hall is surrounded by the arcades of higher levels. In the 1990s, an extension was connected to the main part with a steel-and-glass passageway. On the north side is the University of Applied Arts.

The collections The amazingly rich collections include a fine selection of Jugendstil, Biedermeier and Thonet furniture from Austria. There is a section devoted to objects from the East (textiles, carpets and ceramics), and another part contains European decorative art, including both Venetian and Bohemian glass, Meissen porcelain, and jewellery. The display of works by leading artists of the Wiener Werkstätte on the first floor alone is worth the visit.

Stephansdom

Elaborately carved pulpit in the cathedral (left); the striking tiled roof (right)

St. Stephen's Cathedral has been the spiritual focus of the Viennese people since the Middle Ages—its huge 'Pummerin Bell' rings in the New Year. The great South Tower is affectionately known as the Steffl ('Little Steve').

Ornamentation From the three preceeding Romanesque churches on this site, only the Giant's Door and Heathen Towers (so called because a pagan shrine was supposed to have been here) have survived as part of the Gothic church. Note the striking yellow, green and black chevrons of the tiled roof and a representation of the Habsburg double-headed eagle. Against the north external wall is the pulpit marking the spot where Giovanni Capistrano (1386–1456) preached fiery sermons against the Turks. The cathedral is considered a symbol of endurance, having undergone numerous stages of repair due to the ravages of the Turks, the Napoleonic French and the Allies. All the Federal States contributed to the cathedral's restoration after World War II.

Inside Anton Pilgram's late Gothic pulpit with portraits of the fathers of the church is near the entrance. Above the organ loft of the north aisle is a sculpted self-portrait of Pilgram holding a square and compass. The Gothic vaulting in the Albertine Choir is especially beautiful. Tobias Pock's 1647 baroque altar painting shows the martyrdom of St. Stephen. In the north apse is the exquisite Wiener Neustädter Altar (1447). In the south apse is the magnificent marble tomb of Friedrich III.

THE BASICS

www.stephanskirche.at

➕ F4

✉ Stephansplatz 3

☎ 51 552-35 36

🕐 Church, catacombs, treasury and belltower: Mon–Sat 9–11.30, 1–4.30; Sun 1–4.30. South tower: daily 9–5.30

🚇 U1, U3 to Stephansplatz

🚌 Bus 1A, 2A

♿ Main church: good

💶 Church: free; choir: moderate (guided tour only); catacombs, belltower, treasury, south tower: inexpensive

❓ Evening tours in English with roof walk Jun–Sep Sat 5.30 (meet at south tower reception, expensive)

HIGHLIGHTS

● Pilgram's pulpit
● Tomb of Prince Eugene of Savoy, Kreuzkapelle
● 'Pummerin Bell'
● Nicolas van Leyden's tomb of Friedrich III (1440–93)

More to See

ANNAKIRCHE

An intimate little gem of baroque architecture with Daniel Gran's ceiling fresco of the Immaculate Conception. In the side chapel is a beautiful Gothic carving of Mary, Jesus and St. Anne by Veit Stoss of Nürnberg.

➕ F5 ✉ Annagasse 3B ☎ 512 47 97 🕐 Daily 9–6 🚇 U1, U3 to Stephansplatz

ARTARIA HAUS

Max Fabiani's Artaria House is one of the most striking Jugendstil buildings in the city.

➕ F4 ✉ Kohlmarkt 9 🚇 U3 to Herrengasse

AUGUSTINERKIRCHE

www.augustinerkirche.at

The historic Church of St. Augustine, the 'parish church' of the Habsburg court, can seem bleak and forbidding. In its Loreto Chapel are preserved the hearts of members of the imperial family. On Sunday Vienna's best-sung masses cheer things up.

➕ F5 ✉ Augustinerstrasse 3 (entrance Josefsplatz) ☎ 533 70 99-350 🕐 Mon–Sat 10–6, Sun 1–6, sung mass Sep–Jun Sun 11 🚇 U1, U2, U4 to Karlsplatz/Oper, U3 to Herrengasse 🚌 Hopper 3A to Albertinaplatz ♿ Church only 💶 Inexpensive ❓ Tour of Loreto Chapel and Herzgruft after mass Sun

BURGGARTEN

The vast Jugendstil glasshouse built by Friedrich Ohmann in 1907 replaced the earliest glass-and-iron structure in Vienna (1826).

➕ E5 ✉ Opernring 🕐 Apr–end Oct daily 6am–dusk; Nov–end Mar 6.30am–dusk 🚋 Trams 1, 2, D, J to Burgring

DONNER BRUNNEN

This is a copy of Georg Raphael Donner's Providentia Fountain, which stands in the Belvedere (▷ 82–83). Maria Theresa disapproved of the nude figures. The water nymphs symbolize the rivers of Lower Austria.

➕ F5 ✉ Neuer Markt 🚇 U1, U3 to Stephansplatz

ESPERANTO MUSEUM

A unique collection featuring invented languages. It covers everything from

Annakirche

Detail of the façade of Artaria House

philosophical considerations to terminology, the planning of new languages and intervention in existing ones.

🔢 E4 ✉ Mollard Palace, Herrengasse 9 ☎ 534 10-731 🕐 Mon–Wed, Fri–Sat 10–2, Thu 3–7 🚇 U3 to Herrengasse 💶 Inexpensive

GLOBENMUSEUM

The historic globes in the collection of the Austrian National Library (in the same building as the Esperanto Museum, above) are unique. The oldest one dates back to 1536, but the most precious items are the 10 globes by Venetian Vicenzo Coronelli from the early 18th century. There are also globes featuring the moon and the planets.

🔢 E4 ✉ Mollard Palace, Herrengasse 9 ☎ 534 10-710 🕐 Mon–Wed, Fri–Sat 10–2, Thu 3–7 💶 Inexpensive

HAUS DER MUSIK

www.houseofmusic.at
Vienna's interactive sound museum is well worth a visit. The approach is practical and participatory, so visitors get to compose their own waltz, conduct, or even play instruments. A far cry from musty notes in glass cases and faded artwork on walls. A good restaurant (Cantino) and café provide refreshment.

🔢 F5 ✉ Seilerstätte 30 ☎ 516 48 🕐 Daily 10–10 🚋 Trams D, 1, 2,71 to Schwarzenbergplatz ♿ Good 💶 Expensive

JESUITENKIRCHE

Andrea Pozzo designed this extremely ornate church in the early 18th century. It belonged to the adjacent university over which the Jesuits gained control in 1622. From this base the Jesuits drove forward the Counter-Reformation in Vienna.

🔢 G4 ✉ Dr-Ignaz-Seipel-Platz 1 ☎ 512 52 32 🕐 Daily 7–6.30 🚇 U3 to Stubentor

KARLSPLATZ PAVILIONS

Otto Wagner, the great Secession architect, designed the City Transit Railway. The finest stations are the two on Karlsplatz (1898) and the

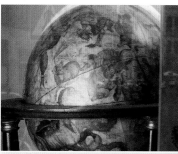

An exhibit in the Globenmuseum

Donner Fountain

emperor's own at Schönbrunn.
🚩 F6 ✉ Karlsplatz 🕐 Tue–Sun 9–noon.
Closed 1 Nov–31 Mar 🚇 U1, U2, U4 to
Karlsplatz

LIPIZZANER MUSEUM WIEN
www.lipizzaner.at
Photographs, antique tack, uniforms
and videos, and displays on the training of the Lipizzaners, plus a peek at
the horses in their stalls.
🚩 F4 ✉ Stallburg/Hofburg Reitschulgasse
2 ☎ 525 24-2502 🕐 Daily 9–6. Tours by
arrangement 🚇 U3 to Herrengasse
🖐 Inexpensive

LOBKOWITZ-PALAIS
The present impressive façade is by
Johann Bernhard Fischer von Erlach.
Beethoven's Eroica Symphony was
given its first performance here in
1804, and during the Congress of
Vienna many famous balls were held.
The Austrian Theatre Museum is here.
🚩 F5 ✉ Lobkowitzplatz 2 ☎ 525
24-3460 🕐 Tue–Sun 10–6, Wed 10–8
🚇 U1, U2, U4 to Karlsplatz/Oper
🖐 Moderate

MOZARTHAUS
www.mozarthausvienna.at
Visit Mozart's lodgings where he wrote
The Marriage of Figaro. No contemporary furniture has survived, but there
is a vivid and entertaining presentation
of his life and times. The audio guide
includes examples of his music.
🚩 G4 ✉ Domgasse 5 ☎ 512 17 91
🕐 Daily 10–7 🍴 Café on premises
🚇 U1, U3 to Stephansplatz 🦽 Good
🖐 Expensive. Reduced ticket includes Haus
der Musik ❓ Museum shop

ÖSTERREICHISCHES
POSTSPARKASSENAMT
The functionalism of Otto Wagner's
Austrian Post Office Savings Bank
(built between 1910 and 1912) made
it seem far in advance of its time.
🚩 H4 ✉ Georg-Coch-Platz ☎ 534 53-
33088 🕐 Mon–Wed, Fri 8–3, Thu 8–5.30
🚇 U1, U4 to Schwedenplatz 🚊 Trams 1, 2
on the Ring to Julius-Raab-Platz 🖐 Moderate

PETERSKIRCHE
The most striking aspect of the lovely
baroque St. Peter's Church is the way

*Otto Wagner's Pavilions
on Karlsplatz*

Mozarthaus

the architects, Gabriele Montani and Lukas von Hildebrandt, fitted it into a space so narrow that it looks almost as if it had been poured into a mould.

➕ F4 ✉ Petersplatz 6 ☎ 533 64 33 🕐 Mon–Fri 7–7, Sat–Sun 9–7 🚇 U1, U3 to Stephansplatz 🚌 Hopper 2A ♿ None 🎫 Free

STAATSOPER

The State Opera reopened in 1955 with a performance of Beethoven's *Fidelio*; appropriately enough, the last performance before it closed in 1944 was Wagner's *Götterdämmerung* (*Twilight of the Gods*). It remains one of the world's top opera stages.

➕ F5 ✉ Opernring 2 ☎ 51 444 🚇 U1, U2, U4 to Oper

STADTPARK

Laid out in 1863 on the old River Wien causeway, the park is packed with monuments to the composers and artists of 19th-century Vienna.

➕ G5 ✉ Stubenring 🕐 Daily 8am–dusk 🚇 U3 to Stubentor, U4 to Stadtpark 🚌 Trams 1, 2

STRAUSS DENKMAL

The preferred statue of the Viennese Waltz King (▷ picture, below).

➕ G5 ✉ Stadtpark 🚌 Trams 1, 2 to Weihburggasse

UHRENMUSEUM

The first of its kind in the world, the Clock Museum covers three floors of Obizzi Palace and houses more than 3,000 exhibits from the 15th to the 20th centuries. Many are unique, including an amazingly complicated astronomical clock—one of its hands requires 20,904 years to make one complete revolution!

➕ F4 ✉ Schulhof 2 (alley flanking Am Hof church) ☎ 533 22 65 🕐 Tue–Sun 9–4.30 🚇 U1, U3 to Stephansplatz 🚌 Hopper 2A ♿ None 🎫 Inexpensive ❓ Tours

WIENFLUSS

Just behind the Strauss Monument, the River Wien leaves its covered channel and emerges through a Secessionist framework designed by Friedrich Ohmann.

➕ H5 ✉ Stadtpark 🚇 U4 to Stadtpark

Strauss Monument

Old Vienna Walk

A walk round the historic Innere Stadt gives you the chance to see some of Vienna's best-known sights and linger in its coffeehouses.

DISTANCE: 3.5km (2.2 miles) **ALLOW:** 2 hours

START

BURGRING
✚ E5 🚇 U3 to Volkstheater

1 Start at the Burgtor on the Ringstrasse. Walk through this triumphal arch into the Heldenplatz. On your right is the Neue Hofburg, containing the National Library and two museums.

2 Continue through the arches into the main courtyard ('In der Burg') of the Hofburg (▷ 26–27). Through the Schweizertor (Swiss Gate) on the south side, the Burgkapelle and the sacred and profane treasuries (Schatzkammer) are reached.

3 From the main courtyard approach the Michaelertor and the entrance to the Imperial Apartments. Exiting onto Michaelerplatz, turn right for Josefsplatz.

4 Head along Augustinerstrasse, passing the Augustinerkirche (▷ 32), then the Albertina (▷ 24), on your right. Behind the Staatsoper (▷ 35) you will see Hotel Sacher (▷ 112).

END

BURGRING
✚ E5 🚇 U3 to Volkstheater

8 Proceed along the Heidenschuss through the Freyung (▷ 25), and turn left through the Ferstel arcade. Emerging on Herrengasse, walk back (left) to the Hofburg's Michaelertor.

7 Walk west along the Graben past the Plague Column and the Peterskirche (▷ 35) on your right. Continue west along picturesque Naglergasse to the southwestern edge of Am Hof.

6 Then turn left into Seilerstätte and left again into Himmelpfort-gasse. At Kärntner Strasse turn right and continue to Stephansplatz and St. Stephen's Cathedral (▷ 31). Opposite is the modern Haas-Haus (1990), by Hans Hollein.

5 Beyond it turn left into Kärntner Strasse, Vienna's premier shopping precinct. Turn right down Annagasse, for the baroque Annakirche (▷ 32).

Shopping

ALTMANN & KÜHNE
The maker of Vienna's best chocolates and the most creative candy.
F4 Graben 30
533 09 27 Mon–Fri 9–6.30, Sat 10–5 U1, U3 to Stephansplatz

ARCADIA OPERA SHOP
The shop for serious opera buffs, staffed by enthusiasts. Next to the opera (▷ 35).
F5 Kärntner Strasse 40
513 95 68 Mon–Sat 9.30–7, Sun 10–7 U1, U2, U4 to Karlsplatz/Oper

AUGARTEN
Porcelain with floral designs produced in Vienna at the factory in the park of the same name (▷ 100).
F4 Stock-im-Eisen-Platz 3 512 14 94
Mon–Fri 10–6.30, Sat 10–6 U1, U3 to Stephansplatz

BRITISH BOOKSHOP
An institution in Vienna. Large selection of books in English, plenty of Austriaca and stacks of novels and history books. Good summer sales bargains. Also at Mariahilferstrasse 4.
G5 Weihburggasse 24
512 19 45 Mon–Fri 9.30–6.30, Sat 9.30–6 Trams 1, 2 to Weihburggasse

C. BEDNARCZYK
Specialist in 18th-century pieces. Paintings, glass, porcelain and silver.

F4 Dorotheergasse 12
512 44 45 Mon–Fri 10–6, Sat 10–1 U1, U2, U4 to Karlsplatz/Oper

DERBY-HANDSCHUHE
Devoted entirely to gloves. The fact that this store remains in business may have something to do with Viennese winters.
F5 Plankengasse 5
512 57 03 Mon–Fri 10–6 U1, U3 to Stephansplatz

DOBLINGER
Mecca for music-lovers and performers: sheet music, books, instruments and CDs.
F4 Dorotheergasse 10
515 03 Mon–Fri 9.30–6.30, Sat 10–1 U1, U3 to Stephansplatz

DOROTHEUM
www.dorotheum.com
An auction house founded in the 18th century in an old convent. You can find everything from the worthless to the priceless, some items marked for direct sale.
F5 Dorotheergasse 17
515 60-226 Art auctions: see website. Exhibitions of objects: Mon–Fri 10–6, Sat 9–5 U1, U2, U4 to Karlsplatz/Oper

DUFT UND KULTUR
This shop has lovely smells to sweeten any room of the house from Africa and the Orient.
F4 Tuchlauben 17
532 39 60 Mon–Fri 10–6.30, Sat 10–5 U1, U3 to Stephansplatz

EMI AUSTRIA
Solid selection in all departments; especially strong on opera and classical music.
F5 Kärntner Strasse 30
512 36 75 Mon–Fri 9.30–6.30, Sat 9.30–5 U1, U2, U4 to Karlsplatz/Oper

FREYTAG & BERNDT
Travel bookshop stocking English titles, especially books on Central Europe. Unrivalled selection of maps and street plans.
F4 Kohlmarkt 9
533 86 85 Mon–Fri 9–7, Sat 9–6 U3 to Herrengasse

FRICK AM GRABEN
Primarily literature, with a small English department.

Paperbacks and children's books are strong points.
⊞ F4 ⊠ Graben 27 ☎ 533 19 14 🕒 Mon–Fri 9–7, Sat 10–6 🚇 U1, U3 to Stephansplatz

FRICK IN DER KÄRNTNER STRASSE

The best shop for books on architecture and the decorative arts, with material on Viennese art and architecture.
⊞ F5 ⊠ Kärntner Strasse 30 ☎ 513 73 64 🕒 Mon–Fri 9–7, Sat 9.30–6 🚇 U1, U2, U4 to Karlsplatz/Oper or U1, U3 to Stephansplatz

GALERIE ERNST HILGER

Contemporary Austrian art. Eleven special exhibitions each year.
⊞ F4 ⊠ Dorotheergasse 12 ☎ 512 53 15 🕒 Tue–Fri 10–6 (Thu 10–8), Sat 10–4 🚇 U1, U3 to Stephansplatz

GALERIE HEIKE CURTZE

This gallery sells work by some of Austria's leading modern artists.
⊞ G5 ⊠ Seilerstätte 15 ☎ 512 93 75 🕒 Tue–Fri 11–6, Sat 12–4 🚇 U1, U3 to Stephansplatz

GALERIE NÄCHST ST. STEPHAN

Avant-garde art from Austria and abroad.
⊞ G4 ⊠ Grünangergasse 1–2 ☎ 512 12 66 🕒 Mon–Fri 11–6, Sat 11–4 🚇 U1, U3 to Stephansplatz

GALERIE NEBEHAY

Author, scholar and collector Christian Nebehay is a leading expert on Klimt and Schiele. His shop also sells old prints and antiquarian books, as well as his own (very useful) books on his specialist field—early-20th-century art.
⊞ F5 ⊠ Annagasse 18 ☎ 512 18 01 🕒 Mon–Fri 9–1, Sat 2–6 🚇 U1, U2, U4 to Karlsplatz/Oper

GALERIE WOLFRUM

The specialist shop for art books, with an excellent print department. Very knowledgeable staff.
⊞ F5 ⊠ Augustinerstrasse 10 ☎ 512 53 98 🕒 Mon–Fri 10–6, Sat 10–5 🚇 U1, U2, U4 to Karlsplatz/Oper

GEA

Shoes in a laid-back style. A local specialty is the

SACHERTORTE

The origin of Sachertorte is so hotly disputed that there have been lawsuits between rival claimants. Those who want authenticity buy at Sacher (⊠ Philharmoniker-strasse 4 ☎ 514 56-853 🕒 Mon–Sat 9am–11pm, Sun 3–6pm. They will also mail). The Hotel Imperial (▷ 112) also offers (to a different recipe) an Imperial Torte. On the other hand, you can buy a perfectly acceptable Sachertorte for much less at any branch of Aida (▷ 43).

Waldviertler ankle boot.
⊞ G5 ⊠ Himmelpfortgasse 26 ☎ 512 19 67 🕒 Mon–Fri 10–6, Sat 10–5 🚇 U1, U3 to Stephansplatz

HAAS & HAAS

A stylish gift shop that stocks candles, dried flowers and delicate ornaments. Café on the premises.
⊞ F5 ⊠ Stephansplatz 4 ☎ 512 26 66 🕒 Mon–Fri 9–6.30, Sat 9–6 🚇 U1, U3 to Stephansplatz

J. & L. LOBMEYR

The famous glassware is still made to the 19th-century neo-baroque and neo-Renaissance design. Above the shop is a small exhibition of J. & L. Lobmeyr's early work.
⊞ F5 ⊠ Kärntner Strasse 26 ☎ 512 05 08 🕒 Mon–Fri 10–7, Sat 10–6 🚇 U1, U3 to Stephansplatz

JULIUS MEINL AM GRABEN

A fine grocer with a superb delicatessen counter and a café, bars and a very expensive restaurant (▷ 45) all with different hours from the shop.
⊞ F4 ⊠ Graben 19 ☎ 532 33 34 🕒 Mon–Wed 8.30–7.30, Thu–Fri 8–7.30, Sat 9–6 🚇 U1, U3 to Stephansplatz

KNIZE

Exclusive men's tailors also notable for the 1913 façade and the interior designed by Adolf Loos.

📍 F4 ✉ Graben 13
☎ 512 21 19 🕐 Mon–Fri
9.30–6, Sat 10–5 🚇 U1, U3
to Stephansplatz

KÖCHERT

Jewellers to the royal and imperial court since 1814, this reputable shop is elegant and restrained.
📍 F5 ✉ Neuer Markt 15
☎ 512 58 28 🕐 Mon–Fri
10–6, Sat 10–5 🚇 U1, U3 to Stephansplatz

METZGER

Honey cake and candles.
📍 F4 ✉ Stephansplatz 7
☎ 512 34 33 🕐 Mon–Fri
9–7, Sat 9–6 🚇 U1, U3 to Stephansplatz

ÖSTERREICHISCHE WERKSTÄTTEN

The wide range of glass ornaments and gifts, with Secessionist designs and attractive enamel make lovely gifts, but be prepared for the aggressive sales people.
📍 F4 ✉ Kärntner Strasse 6
☎ 512 24 18 🕐 Mon–Fri
10–6.30, Sat 10–6 🚇 U1, U3 to Stephansplatz

RASPER & SÖHNE

A highly respected emporium for glass, porcelain and cutlery, although some of the styles are an acquired taste.
📍 F4 ✉ Habsburgergasse 1A ☎ 534 33 🕐 Mon–Fri
10–6.30, Sat 10–5 🚇 U1, U3 to Stephansplatz

RESI HAMMERER

Here you'll find *Trachtenmode* as well as haute couture. The owner skied on the Austrian national team.
📍 F5 ✉ Kärntner Strasse
29–31 ☎ 512 69 52
🕐 Mon–Fri 9.30–6, Sat 10–5
🚇 U1, U3 to Stephansplatz

ROBERT HORN

A cult shop offering fine leather briefcases, handbags, wallets and lots more for the chic man or woman about town.
📍 F4 ✉ Bräunerstrasse 7
☎ 513 82 94 🕐 Mon–Fri
10–6.30, Sat 10–5 🚇 U1, U3 to Stephansplatz

SCHÖNBICHLER

The Viennese come here to buy their English marmalade and tea, Scotch whisky and Christmas pudding.
📍 G4 ✉ Wollzeile 4
☎ 512 18 16 🕐 Mon–Fri
9–6.30, Sat 9–5 🚇 U1, U3 to Stephansplatz

ANTIQUES SHOPS

While other shops are scattered around the whole district, antiques shops are concentrated in the side-streets running from Graben to the Hofburg. In the Bräunerstrasse, Dorotheergasse and Spiegelgasse you will find an ever-changing display of what has survived from the collections of the Viennese art-loving nobility and middle class. In the Dorotheum (▷ 38), you can also participate in an auction.

STEFFL

Futuristic shop interior full of top labels. Also a floor devoted to cosmetics. Media café, bar and restaurant.
📍 F5 ✉ Kärntner Strasse 19
☎ 514 31-0 🕐 Mon–Fri
9.30–7, Sat 9.30–6 🚇 U1, U3 to Stephansplatz

VIENNA BAG SHOP

www.vienna-bag.at
This unusual shop sells the last cry in stylish handbags made from glass fibre, and mostly in dazzling hues.
📍 G4 ✉ Bäckerstrasse 7
☎ 513 11 84 🕐 Mon
10.30–6, Tue–Fri 10.30–6
🚇 U1, U3 to Stephansplatz

WIENER INTERIEUR

Compact shop specializing in fine examples of smaller Jugendstil and art deco objects.
📍 F4 ✉ Dorotheergasse 14
☎ 512 28 98 🕐 Mon–Fri
10–6, Sat 10–1 🚇 U1, U2, U4, to Karlsplatz/Oper

WOKA

If you're looking for something with the appearance of the Wiener Werkstätte to take home, a reproduction lamp from this high-quality workshop—in business since 1978—may be the answer. Great style.
📍 G4 ✉ Singerstrasse 16
☎ 513 29 12 🕐 Mon–Fri
10–6, Sat 10–5 🚇 U1, U3 to Stephansplatz

Entertainment and Nightlife

BADESCHIFF
www.badeschiff.at
Forget the ocean cruise: Vienna has its very own ship pool in the Donaukanal downstream from Schwedenplatz. The boat is narrow, but 30m (98ft) long, and remains open as long as the warm weather holds. The adjoining second ship with gastronomy and cultural offers is open year-round.
🚇 H3 ☒ Franz-Josefs-Kai between Schwedenplatz and Urania 🕐 Pool summer 8am–midnight 🚇 U1, U4 to Schwedenplatz 🚃 Trams 1, 2, N to Schwedenplatz

DEUTSCHMEISTER
www.deutschmeister.at
Recently the successor of Austria's most famous regimental band revived the tradition of regular concerts in the main courtyard of the Hofburg. The ceremony starts at 11am, with a march from the Graben, down the Kohlmarkt and across the Michaelerplatz to the monument of Emperor Francis. Here a concert of Austrian march music is given. Shortly before noon the band returns to the Graben where a farewell is played.
🚇 E4 ☒ In der Burg 🕐 0664-43 45 467 🕐 May to mid-Oct Sat 11 🚇 U3 Herrengasse 🚃 Trams 1, 2, D, J to Dr-Karl-Renner-Ring; bus 3A to Heldenplatz or Michaelerplatz

EDEN BAR
www.edenbar.at
Elegant dress code and live music are characteristic of this exclusive bar in the shadow of St. Stephen's. To be a regular guest at the Eden Bar stamps you as a member of Vienna's high society.
🚇 F4 ☒ Liliengasse 2 🕐 512 74 50 🕐 Mon–Sat 9pm–4am 🚇 U1, U3 to Stephansplatz

ETABLISSEMENT RONACHER
www.musicalvienna.at/theater
This wonderful old variety theatre, with an exotic late 19th-century interior, has reopened after a long period of darkness. Its

NIGHT MUSIC

You can now hear most types of jazz regularly in Vienna. In summer there is a jazz festival held partly in the hallowed Staatsoper (▷ 35), and there is an open-air festival on the Donauinsel (Danube Island) in July. Performances generally start at 9pm but check the current Wien Programm (available at all Tourist Information Bureaux). The night scene has grown livelier and the *Bermuda Dreieck* (Bermuda Triangle, ▷ 13) is a magnet for gilded youth. You will find there idiosyncratic bars, trendy restaurants, discos, beer cellars, live music and cabaret.

schedule remains unpredictable—from a spectacular à la André Heller to a Broadway musical.
🚇 G5 ☒ Seilerstätte 9 🕐 58830-0 🕐 Reopening in 2008 🚇 U1, U3 to Stephansplatz, U4 to Stadtpark

KAMMERSPIELE
www.josefstadt.org
This subsidiary stage of the Theater in der Josefstadt puts on plays, lighter fare—often comedies and farces, not infrequently recycled London West End hits.
🚇 G4 ☒ Rotenturmstrasse 20 🕐 42 700-64 🚇 U1, U4 to Schwedenplatz

KURSALON
www.kursalonwien.at
The Strauss summer festival takes place inside the Kursalon in the Stadtpark (originally a place where bourgeois park visitors could sample the health-giving spa water).
🚇 G5 ☒ Johannesgasse 33 🕐 513 24 77 🚇 U4 to Stadtpark 🚃 Trams 1, 2 to Weihburggasse

NIGHTFLY'S CLUB
www.nightflys.at
An intimate cellar bar where you'll hear golden oldies, from Glenn Miller to Frank Sinatra.
🚇 F4 ☒ Dorotheergasse 14 🕐 512 99 79 🕐 Summer 6pm–3am, winter 8pm–3am 🚇 U1, U3 to Stephansplatz

ÖSTERREICHISCHES FILMMUSEUM

www.filmmuseum.at

The dedicated Austrian Film Museum has kept this shrine to the movies alive. Pay the low membership fee, then a modest entrance charge.

➕ F5 ✉ Augustinerstrasse 1 (Albertina) ☎ 533 70 54 🕐 Mon–Thu 10–6, Fri 10–1 🚇 U1, U2, U4 to Karlsplatz/Oper

ROTER ENGEL

www.roterengel.at

'The Red Angel' exemplifies the best of the Bermuda Dreieck. It calls itself a *Wein und Liederbar* (wine and song bar) and serves drinkable wines with cheeses. It also has folk and rhythm and blues evenings.

➕ G3 ✉ Rabensteig 5 ☎ 535 41 05 🕐 Sun–Wed 4pm–2am, Thu–Sat 4pm–4am 🚇 U1, U4 to Schwedenplatz 🚊 Trams 1, 2 to Schwedenplatz

STAATSOPER

www.wiener-staatsoper.at

The Vienna State Opera (▷ 35) ranks among the world's top opera houses, and this is mainly due to its wonderful orchestra, from which the members of the private Wiener Philharmoniker are elected. Viennese music lovers cheer their preferred singers extravagantly. But they can also be merciless, and it is said that being director of the State Opera is the most brutal job in the country. Among the celebrities who held the post were Gustav Mahler, Richard Strauss, Herbert von Karajan and Lorin Maazel.

The building is not as impressive as you would imagine, because bombs destroyed most of the interior in World War II. The ceremonial staircase and the front foyers have been restored.

➕ F5 ✉ Opernring 2 ☎ 51444-2250 🚇 U1, U2, U4 to Karlsplatz/Oper 🚊 Trams 1, 2, D, J, 62, 65, Badner Bahn to Kärntner Ring/Oper

STADTFEST

www.stadtfestwien.at

On a Saturday in spring,

MUSICAL TRADITION

Music has been part of the city's culture from earliest times. In the mid-18th century Haydn and then Mozart began to displace the long-dominant Italian composers in public esteem. The 19th century was also rich in musical talent, some of it imported (Beethoven, Brahms) but much homegrown (Schubert, Bruckner, Hugo Wolf, Strauss father and son and Mahler). Later, Arnold Schönberg pioneered the 12-tone system, while his erstwhile-pupils, such as Alban Berg and Anton von Webern, made the 'Second Viennese School' world famous.

---

the Inner City hosts many different kinds of events connected with the City Festival. Organized by the conservative People's Party, it is their answer to the Social Democrats' Festival on the Danube Island (Donauinsel).

➕ F4 ✉ Inner City 🕐 One Saturday in spring 🚇 U1, U3 to Stephansplatz

STRANDBAR HERRMANN

www.strandbarherrmann.at

Situated where the River Wien debouches into the Danube Canal, this is Vienna's first Beach Club with deck-chairs, dining and DJ music in the evening. A very informal place mainly frequented by the younger generation. To go swimming, you will have to cross the bridge to the Urania and walk a short distance upstream to board the Badeschiff (▷ 41).

➕ H3 ✉ Donaukanal-Promenade/Urania 🕐 Daily May–end Sep 10am–2am 🚊 Trams 1, 2, N to Julius-Raab-Platz

WIENER KAMMEROPER

www.wienerkammeroper.at

A seedbed for talent for the Volksoper, Staatsoper or abroad. The schedule includes many lesser-known operas, sometimes abridged. A small, intimate space.

➕ G4 ✉ Fleischmarkt 24 ☎ 512 01 00 🚇 U1, U4 to Schwedenplatz

Restaurants

PRICES

Prices are approximate, based on a 3-course meal for one person.

€€€ over €40
€€   €20–€40
€   under €20

AIDA (€)

It's cramped, but the coffee and cakes are good.
🔹 F4 ✉ Singerstrasse 1
☎ 512 29 77 🕐 Mon–Sat 7am–8pm, Sun 9–8 🚇 U1, U3 to Stephansplatz
Also at: Bognergasse 3, Rotenturmstrasse 24, Wollzeile 28

AUGUSTINERKELLER (€€)

Good Austrian and Viennese food, plus local wines. A bit touristy.
🔹 F5 ✉ Augustinerstrasse 1
☎ 533 10 26 🕐 Daily 11–midnight, Sat 11am–1am
🚇 U1, U2, U4 to Karlsplatz/Oper 🚌 Bus 3A to Albertinaplatz

BEIM CZAAK (€)

A traditional *Beisl* tucked away in a quiet corner of the Innere Stadt. Viennese cuisine, but with emphasis on its Czech origins (dumplings to the fore!).
🔹 G4 ✉ Postgasse 15
☎ 513 72 15 🕐 Mon–Sat 11–midnight 🚇 U1, U4 to Schwedenplatz

DA BIZI (€–€€)

A self-service system allows you to assemble the menu of your choice.
🔹 G4 ✉ Rotenturmstrasse 4
☎ 513 38 05 🕐 Daily 11am–midnight 🚇 U1, U3 to Stephansplatz

DEMEL (€€–€€€)

Founded in 1776 close to the now-demolished Burgtheater on Michaelerplatz. Christoph Demel took over in 1857, and it remained in the family until Anna Demel's death in 1956. The staff were traditionally recruited from a convent in Währing and decked out in black uniforms with white frills. The lavish interior is a restoration dating from the 1930s.
🔹 F4 ✉ Kohlmarkt 14
☎ 535 17 17 🕐 Daily 10–7
🚇 U3 to Herrengasse 🚌 Bus 2A to Michaelerplatz

FOOD FROM AROUND THE WORLD

Although Vienna has had a large international community since the 1970s, the choice of non-Viennese cooking is not as great as you might expect in a capital city. True, pizza and pasta are ubiquitous, and the number of Chinese and Japanese restaurants is growing; yet there are surprisingly few French restaurants of repute, the Greek and Spanish selection is disappointing, and the cuisines of some other territories are virtually unknown. The list here reflects the relative choice available.

DIGLAS (€)

Founded in 1923, it was a comparative latecomer to the coffeehouse scene. Its most famous regular customer was the composer Franz Lehár.
🔹 G4 ✉ Wollzeile 10
☎ 512 57 65-0 🕐 Daily 7am–midnight 🚇 U1, U3 to Stephansplatz

DO & CO (€€€)

www.doco.com
The restaurant's superb location in Hans Hollein's Haas Haus offers a view of the cathedral from the best tables. The excellent cuisine includes Far and Middle East cooking mixed with local tradition. The owner, Attila Dogudan, runs the British Museum Gourmet Restaurant.
🔹 F4 ✉ Stephansplatz 12
☎ 535 39 69 🕐 Daily 12–3, 6–midnight 🚇 U1, U3 to Stephansplatz

ESTERHAZYKELLER (€)

The Esterhazys gave free wine to the populace here during the 1683 Turkish siege. The wine is no longer free but it's still very good value, as is the simple food.
🔹 F4 ✉ Haarhof 1 (off Wallnerstrasse) ☎ 533 34 82
🕐 Mon–Fri 11–11, Sat–Sun 4–11 🚇 U3 to Herrengasse

FABIOS (€€€)

www.fabios.at
When opened in 2002, Fabio Giacobello's designer restaurant became the

most trendy of Vienna's top-level eateries almost overnight. The glass-façade can be removed, weather permitting. Its creative cuisine has made it a celebrity hot spot.

➕ F4 ✉ Tuchlauben 6 ☎ 532 22 22 🕓 Mon–Sat 10–1. Open on hols 🚇 U1, U3 to Stephansplatz

FIGLMÜLLER (€€)

Always crowded, but good value, with huge schnitzels and a choice of wines by the glass. No beer.

➕ G4 ✉ Wollzeile 5 ☎ 512 61 77 🕓 Daily 11am–11.30pm. Closed Aug 🚇 U1, U3 to Stephansplatz
Also at: ➕ G4
✉ Bäckerstrasse 6 ☎ 512 17 60 🕓 Daily 12–12. Closed Jul 🚇 U1, U3 to Stephansplatz

HAAS & HAAS (€€)

www.haas-haas.at
An annex to the Haas & Haas Tea House behind St. Stephen's Cathedral, this restaurant excels with a small, but fine menu and good Austrian wines. It also has a delightful garden in the courtyard of the Teutonic Order.

➕ G4 ✉ Stephansplatz 4 ☎ 512 26 66 🕓 Mon–Fri 8–8, Sun 8–6.30 🚇 U1, U3 to Stephansplatz

HEINER (€€)

The branch overlooking Kärntner Strasse is excellent, but the little Biedermeier interior of Heiner in the Wollzeile is irresistible; a doll's house

atmosphere. The cakes and pastries are really superb and the coffee good; fine handmade chocolates, too. Special goodies for diabetics are available.

➕ F5 ✉ Kärntner Strasse 21–3 ☎ 512 68 63 🕓 Mon–Sat 8.30–7.30, Sun 10–7.30 🚇 U1, U3 to Stephansplatz
Also at: ➕ G4 ✉ Wollzeile 9 ☎ 512 23 43-16 🕓 Mon–Sat 8.30–7, Sun and hols 10–7 🚇 U1, U3 to Stephansplatz

HUMMERBAR (€€€)

Vienna's most renowned fish restaurant with the famous *Hummerbar* (lobster bar). Downstairs is a more modest Turkish restaurant.

➕ F5 ✉ Mahlerstrasse 9 ☎ 512 88 43 🕓 Mon–Sat 12–12 🚇 U1, U2, U4 to Karlsplatz/Oper

---

ALTERNATIVES

Apart from the Nordsee chain (▷ 45), there are a growing number of possibilities for serious fish eaters. For the freshest and best, you have to be prepared to dig deep in the pocket. The pizza trade expands even faster than hamburger joints in this part of the world, and there is now a good choice of places in central Vienna serving freshly-made pizzas. There are even, in a city of mainly meat-eaters, some vegetarian restaurants.

ILONA–STÜBERL (€€)

www.ilonastueberl.at
Excellent value; stuffed cabbage, goulash and other Hungarian fare.

➕ F4 ✉ Bräunerstrasse 2 ☎ 533 90 29 🕓 Oct–end Mar Tue–Sun 12–11, Apr–end Sep daily 11.30–11.30 🚇 U1, U3 to Stephansplatz

KERN'S BEISEL (€€)

www.kernbeisl.at
A wonderful place to experience honest Austrian cooking, with friendly service. A major plus is the wide selection of Austrian wines by the glass and spirits (there is a small bar at the back). Unpretentious restaurateurship at its best.

➕ F4 ✉ Kleeblattgasse 4 (off Tuchlauben) ☎ 533 91 88 🕓 Mon–Fri 9am–11pm 🚇 U1, U3 to Stephansplatz

KORNAT (€€–€€€)

www.kornat.at
This Croatian restaurant serves fish flown in fresh from the Dalmatian coast with wines from Hvar and Korcula.

➕ G3 ✉ Marc-Aurel-Strasse 8 ☎ 535 65 18 🕓 Mon–Sat 11.30–3, 6–midnight 🚇 U1, U4 to Schwedenplatz

KORSO BEI DER OPER (€€€)

Many consider this elegant restaurant in the Hotel Bristol the best in town, with the finest Viennese cuisine.

➕ F5 ✉ Mahlerstrasse 2 ☎ 515 16-546 🕓 Daily 7pm–1am, Sun–Fri 12–3pm.

Closed Aug  U1, U2, U4 to Karlsplatz/Oper

Closed 24–26 Dec  U3 to Stubentor

9–midnight  U1, U2, U4 to Karlsplatz/Oper

MEINL AM GRABEN (€€€)

A discreet gourmet-stop in the only remaining branch of quality grocer Meinl. The best of Austrian cooking in an informal atmosphere; fabulous wines.

F4 ✉ Graben 19 ☎ 532 33 34-6000 ⏱ Mon–Wed 8.30–midnight, Thu–Fri 8–midnight, Sat 9–midnight  U3, U1 to Stephansplatz

NORDSEE (€–€€)

Not just fish-and-chips. You'll find a wide range of seafood dishes and sandwiches with fish fillings. Self-service.

F4 ✉ Kohlmarkt 6 ☎ 533 59 66 ⏱ Daily 10–8; Jul–end Sep 10–9  U1, U3 to Stephansplatz

Also at: Kärntner Strasse 25, Rotenturmstrasse 4

NOVELLI BACARO CON CUCINA (€€€)

When you're tired of pizza and pasta, look to this lovely restaurant with superb Italian fare and wines to match.

F4 ✉ Bräunerstrasse 11 ☎ 513 42 00 ⏱ Mon–Sat 11am–1am  U1, U3 to Stephansplatz

PRÜCKEL (€)

Prückel has piano music on Monday, Wednesday and Friday evenings.

G4 ✉ Stubenring 24/Dr-Karl-Lueger-Platz ☎ 512 61 15 ⏱ Daily 8.30am–10pm.

RIEGI (€€€)

www.riegi.at

Said to be the best Italian restaurant in Vienna, with a famed wine list, and no pizzas.

F4 ✉ Schauflergasse 6 ☎ 532 91 26 ⏱ Tue–Sat 12–3, 6–midnight  U3 to Herrengasse

TIROLERHOF (€)

Coffeehouses were originally for men only, but this one had an exclusively female clientele as early as 1910. Now mixed, it is still preferred among women.

F5 ✉ Führichgrasse 8 (Albertinaplatz) ☎ 512 78 33 ⏱ Mon–Fri 7am–9pm, Sat 7am–2am, Sun, hols

TRZESNIEWSKI (€)

www.trznesniewski.at

Lots of open sandwiches, with toppings of fish, meat, vegetables, poultry and free-range eggs.

F4 ✉ Dorotheergasse 1 ☎ 512 32 91 ⏱ Mon–Fri 8.30–7.30, Sat 9–5  U1, U3 to Stephansplatz

WRENKH (€€)

Exquisite vegetarian cuisine such as wild rice risotto with mushrooms, and Greek fried rice with vegetables, sheep's cheese and olives.

F4 ✉ Bauernmarkt 10 ☎ 533 15 26 ⏱ Daily 12–4, 6–11, Sat, hols 6pm–11pm  U1, U3 to Stephansplatz

ZUM SCHWARZEN KAMEEL (€€–€€€)

www.kameel.at

For a charming Viennese lunch, try the Jugendstil Black Camel.

F4 ✉ Bognergasse 5 ☎ 533 81 25 ⏱ Mon–Sat 8.30am–midnight  U3 to Herrengasse

ZWÖLF-APOSTELKELLER (€)

A student hang-out. Very atmospheric cellars on three levels.

G4 ✉ Sonnenfelsgasse 3 ☎ 512 67 77 ⏱ Daily 4.30pm–midnight  U1, U3 to Stephansplatz

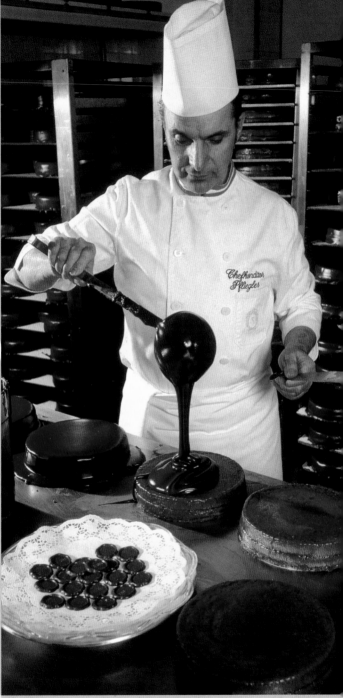

Largely undamaged by World War II, the Ringstrasse is one of Europe's great boulevards. It boasts magnificent edifices created for cultural and political institutions, but also elegant parks and traditional coffeehouses.

Grillparzerstrasse

Museum auf Abruf

Felderstrasse

Wiener Stadt- und Landesbibl

RING

Rathaus

Rathaus- platz

Rathaus- Park

LÖWELSTRASSE

Burgtheater

DR KARL LUEGER

Meinrad- platz

Schottstift

Kaiserin Elisabeth Denkmal

Löwelstrasse

Reichratsstrasse

DR K-RENNER RING

Schmerlingplatz

Parlament

Volksgarten

Ballhaus- platz

Justiz- palast

VOLKSGARTEN STRASSE

Palais Epstein

Heiden- platz

BELLARIASTRASSE

BURGRING

Natur- historisches Museum

Maria-Theresien- platz

Burgtor (Heldentor)

Volks- theater

Volks- Theater

Architektur- zentrum

MUMOK

Kunsthistorisches Museum

MUSEUMSPLATZ

BABENBERGERSTRASSE

OPERNRING

Kunsthalle Wien

MuseumsQuartier

Leopold Museum

Schottenbachgasse

Elisabethstrasse

OPERNGASSE

ZOOM Kindermuseum

Museumsquartier

Nibelungengasse

Dschungel Wien

GETREIDE- MARKT

Schwindgasse gasse

Rahlgasse

Akademie der Bildenden Künste

FRIEDRICHSTRASSE

Strasse St Joseph

Theo- baldgasse

i

Karlsplatz

Interkulttheater

Filgradergasse gasse

STRASSE

Lehár- gasse

Girardigasse

Secession

Theater an der Wien

Kunsthalle Wien project space

Resselgasse

GUMPENDORFER

grubengasse

Alfred- Grünwald- Park

Köstlergasse

WIENZEILE

WIENZEILE

Schauhofergasse

OPERN- GASSE

Paniglgasse

HAUPTSTRASSE

Naschmarkt

Steigergasse

LINKE

RECHTE

SCHLEIFMÜHLGASSE

Mühl-

Schleifmühlgasse

Wagner Apartments

Press- gasse

WIEDNER

KETTENBRÜCKENGASSE

Franzens- gasse

Kettenbrücken-

Heumühl-

gasse

Dritte-Mann- Museum 3mpc gasse

MARGARETENSTRASSE

HAMBURGERSTRASSE

Wehr-

Grün-gasse

gasse

Schubert Sterbehaus

Sterbegasse

E

F

Akademie der Bildenden Künste

Otto Wagner's former apartment (left); statue of Schiller (middle) outside the Academy of Fine Arts (right)

THE BASICS

www.akbild.ac.at

🞧 E6

✉ Schillerplatz 3

☎ 58 816-225

🕐 Tue–Sun 10–4. Closed 1 Jan, 1 May, 1 Nov, 24–25 Dec, 31 Dec

🚇 U1, U2, U4 Karlsplatz/Oper

🚊 Trams 1 and 2 to Babenberger Strasse

♿ Call in advance for access at Makartgasse entrance

💰 Moderate

❓ Audio guide

HIGHLIGHTS

● *Last Judgement*, Hieronymus Bosch

● *Views of Venice*, Antonio Guardi

● *Family in a Courtyard*, Pieter de Hooch

● Sketches for Banqueting House, Whitehall, Rubens

In 1907, Adolf Hitler was denied entry to the Academy of Fine Arts for his poor rendering of human heads. He tried a second time and was rejected by the academy's architecture professor, Otto Wagner, because he lacked the requisite academic qualifications. He later turned to politics.

The building The academy was completed in 1876 by one of the greatest architects of the Ringstrassen era, Theophil Hansen, whose other work includes the classical Parliament, the Stock Exchange and numerous neo-Renaissance palaces. In the middle of the square in front is a statue of the poet Friedrich Schiller (1759–1805). Along the façade are figures from antiquity associated with the fine arts; on the back are allegorical frescos by August Eisenmenger, the academy's Professor for Painting in the late 19th century. Founded in 1692 by the painter Peter von Strudel, the academy numbers among its alumni the painter Friedensreich Hundertwasser, whose spectacular multihued house at Löwengasse, 3rd District is a tourist attraction, and Fritz Wotruba, designer of an extraordinary modern church (▷ 101).

The interior Anselm Feuerbach's ceiling fresco, *Downfall of Titans*, dominates the Basilical Hall; the collection of Dutch Masters is renowned and the graphic art collection, which is due to re-open by the end of 2008, is superb. Few teaching academies possess such a large graphic collection developed over 300 years.

Bust of Schiller (left) on the Burgtheater (right)

Burgtheater

The Burgtheater is Austria's national theatre in all but name. It is regarded as one of the best German-language theatres and appearing on its stage represents the peak of an actor's career.

Origins The name is taken from the court theatre that stood on the edge of the Hofburg (on Michaelerplatz) from the time of Maria Theresa (1741) until 1888.

Architecture This neo-Renaissance building by Karl von Hasenauer and Gottfried Semper opened in 1888, but it was soon altered; so much attention in the design had been paid to architectural proportion and so little to function that some of the boxes faced away from the stage and the acoustics were appalling. An anecdote claimed that 'In the Parliament you can't hear anything, in the Rathaus you can't see anything and in the Burgtheater you can neither see nor hear anything'.

Decorative plan Inside and out, the Burgtheater is a symbolic celebration of the history of drama. On the central façade are monuments to the world's greatest playwrights. On the ceremonial stairways that rise through the two wings toward the auditorium are busts of the great Austrian and German dramatists. Gustav Klimt, his brother Ernst and Franz Matsch decorated the ceilings above the stairway with frescos depicting the history of theatre. Oil portraits of famous Viennese actors and actresses hang on the walls of the foyer.

THE BASICS

www.burgtheater.at
🔲 E4
✉ Dr-Karl-Lueger-Ring
☎ 51444-4140
🎫 Guided tours daily at 3pm from the Ticket Hall. Closed 24 Dec, Good Friday, Jul and Aug except for tours. No tours during afternoon performances
🚇 U2 Schottentor
🚃 Trams 1, 2, D to Burgtheater
♿ Good; by prior arrangement
💰 Moderate

HIGHLIGHTS

Exterior
● View from the Rathaus across Ringstrasse
Interior
● Ceremonial stairway, busts of dramatists
● *Thespiscart*, Gustav Klimt
● *Globe Theatre, London*, Gustav Klimt
● *Theatre at Taormina*, Gustav Klimt
● *Medieval Mystery Theatre*, Ernst Klimt
● *Molière's Le Malade Imaginaire*, Ernst Klimt

Kunsthistorisches Museum

In the Museum of Art History you'll find the Habsburgs' fabulous art collection, acquired over centuries (especially by Emperor Rudolf II and Archdukes Leopold Wilhelm and Ferdinand II).

Origins The German architect Gottfried von Semper planned to continue the sweep of the Neue Hofburg and build a parallel wing on the other side of the Heldenplatz; both wings were to extend across the Ringstrasse, creating a gigantic Imperial Forum of museums. The Museum of Art History and the Natural History Museum facing it are the partial realization of this attempt to bring together the widely dispersed Habsburg treasures. The Museum of Art History contains collections of paintings, Egyptian objects, sculpture, decorative art, coins and medals.

Statue at the entrance of the Museum of Art History; portrait of Ferdinand II; the monument to Maria Theresa stands in the middle of the park; gallery of paintings; a bust on display in the museum (clockwise from far left)

Architectural decoration Both the Museum of Art History and the Natural History Museum opposite are principally the work of Gottfried von Semper; their interiors are by Karl Hasenauer. Between the museums lies a park that is dominated by a monument to Maria Theresa (1740–80). Inside the Museum of Art History, marble and stucco are interspersed with murals; most notable is the ceiling fresco above the main landing, Mihály Munkácsy's *Apotheosis of Art*. Note the dome, which has medallions of collector-emperors. Hasenauer planned showrooms appropriate to their contents; the Egyptian collection, for example, is ornamented with columns from Luxor, a present from the Khedive to the Emperor Franz Josef. Benvenuto Cellini's *Saliera* (*Salt Cellar*), stolen in 2003 and recovered from Lower Austria in 2006, is a gem of Renaissance craftsmanship.

THE BASICS

www.khm.at
✚ E5
✉ Maria-Theresien-Platz
☎ 552 24-0
🕐 Tue–Sun 10–6 (Thu until 9). Closed 24 Dec, shorter hours 1 Jan
🍴 Café in Cupola Hall
🚇 U2 to Museums-Quartier, U3 to Volkstheater
🚊 Trams 1, 2, D, J to Burgring
♿ Good
💰 Expensive
❓ Frequent lectures and special exhibitions

MuseumsQuartier

TOP 25

Cooling off in the MuseumsQuartier (left); Museum of Modern Art (right)

RINGSTRASSE TOP 25

THE BASICS

www.mqw.at

☧ D5

✉ Museumsplatz 1

☎ 523 58 81

🕐 Daily 10–6, Thu until 9

Ⓜ U2 to MuseumsQuartier, U2, U3 to Volkstheater

♿ Good

💶 Expensive (separate tickets)

HIGHLIGHTS

● *Death and Life*, Gustav Klimt

● Self-portrait by Egon Schiele (both in the Leopold Museum)

TIP

● Enjoy excellent traditional Viennese fare at Glacisbeisl restaurant, with an open-air terrace and trendy modern dining room. It is reached up the steps from the MuseumsQuartier (☎ 526 56 60 🕐 Daily 11am–2am, kitchen until 11pm).

Museums located in this quarter occupying the former Imperial Stables include the Kunsthalle and the Museum of Modern Art. The Leopold Museum has a fine collection of works by Gustav Klimt, Egon Schiele and other artists of the period.

Meeting place Originally a futuristic 'Book Tower' was planned to attract passers-by and give the area a distinctive modern counterpoint to the architecture of the former Imperial Stables. But the grandiose concept here ended in compromise: only two museums exceed the height of the baroque stables in front of them. Since 2001, it has become one of the liveliest places in the city. It is central and easy to access. Young people meet there to see the cutting-edge exhibitions in the Kunsthalle at its middle, socialize in one of the restaurants or simply relax on the '*Enzis*' ('Only for Singles?') in the main courtyard—modernistic benches on which you can lie, lean or sit.

The Leopold Museum Numerous cultural institutions here, such as the Architekturzentrum, the Tanzquartier, the Children's Museum and the Museum of Modern Art, attract all kinds of visitors (some of them visit the MUMOK just for the fine view from its top floor). The flagship is definitely the Leopold Museum with its excellent collection of Austrian *fin-de-siècle* art brought together by the collector (and ophthalmologist!) who gave the collection to the nation and is curator for life.

A summer concert (left) in the courtyard of the Rathaus (right)

The 'new' City Hall (Neues Rathaus), built between 1872 and 1883 by architect Friedrich Schmidt, is possibly the finest neo-Gothic building in Vienna. Certainly, the debating chamber would not disgrace a small independent nation.

Inspiration The great buildings along the Ringstrasse, built between the 1860s and 1880s, exemplify the values of Liberalism—industrial modernization, democracy and capitalist enterprise. It is typically Viennese that this vision of the future was expressed in historic symbols. Schmidt chose as his model town halls typical of medieval Flanders. The main inspiration was the Brussels City Hall.

Inside and out The huge façade with its traceried arches over the arcades faces the Ringstrasse; above the arches are loggias and imposing balustrades adorned with statues. Rising from the middle is the 98m (321ft) tower topped by a 3.4m (11ft) copper statue. Inside, the grand staircases, noble promenades and richly decorated halls are a spectacle; don't miss the City Council Chamber and the Ceremonial Hall.

City Council The members of the Vienna City Council double as members of the Vienna Provincial Diet, since Vienna is both a municipality and a Federal State of Austria. Although they have two roles, they are not political chameleons—since 1919 the Rathaus has been a stronghold of Social Democrats, with a break only in the Nazi period and the Clerical-Fascist regime that preceded it.

THE BASICS

www.wien.gv.at/english/cityhall/tours.htm

🟦 D4

✉ Friedrich-Schmidt-Platz 1

☎ 525 50

🕐 Tours: Mon, Wed, Fri 1pm. Closed session days, Good Friday, 24, 31 Dec

🍴 Rathauskeller

Ⓤ U2 Rathaus

🚊 Trams 1 and 2 on the Ringstrasse, D, J

♿ Good; phone or write in advance

🎫 Tour: free (in German only)

❓ Visits by tour only (apply at Stadtinformationszentrum in Schmidthalle)

HIGHLIGHTS

- Statues
- Monument to President Karl Renner
- Opera films in summer; Christmas Market
- The Arkadenhof (arcaded courtyard)

Secession

The Secession's dome of gilded laurel leaves (left); detail of the façade (right)

THE BASICS

www.secession.at
E6
Friedrichstrasse 12
587 53 07
Tue–Sun 10–6 (Thu until 8). Closed 1 May, 1 Nov, 25 Dec
Summer café beside the building
U1, U2, U4 Karlsplatz
Bus 59A
Few
Moderate

HIGHLIGHTS

● Three gorgons over the doorway
● Inscription *Ver Sacrum* (Sacred Spring)
● Dome of gilded laurel leaves
● Picturesque sculpted owls
● Vast flower tubs on tortoise stands
● Statue: *Mark Antony in a Chariot Drawn by Lions* (1900), Arthur Strasser
● *Beethoven Frieze* (1902), Gustav Klimt

In a gesture of defiance toward the art establishment, this exhibition building of revolutionary design was built under the windows of the Academy of Fine Arts. Their motto is inscribed over the entrance: 'To every age its art, to art its freedom'.

Vienna Secession In 1897, frustrated with the increasing conservatism of academic painting in Vienna and its stranglehold over the art market, a group of young artists broke away to form the subsequently famous 'Vienna Secession'. Its elected head was the painter Gustav Klimt, whose *Beethoven Frieze*—an allegorical interpretation of the themes of the Ninth Symphony and a homage to the composer—can be seen here.

Jugendstil Klimt began his career working in the conventional genre of historical painting (exemplified by his work for the Burgtheater, ▷ 51). The Secession's style was associated with Jugendstil, the German version of art nouveau. It is sensuous and decorative, and achieves its best effects in architecture and stained glass.

The exhibition hall The breakaway artists needed a hall both to exhibit their own works and to display avant-garde art from abroad. In 1898, Joseph Maria Olbrich completed the cubelike, towered and windowless Secession Building with a glass roof that provided daylight. The Viennese dubbed it the 'Golden Cabbage' because of its gilded dome of entwined laurel leaves.

More to See

HAUS DES MEERES
www.haus-des-meeres.at

The 'Flakturm' in Esterhazypark, one of six anti-aircraft towers left over from the Nazi hegemony in Vienna, now houses snakes, spiders and crocodiles, and an aquarium. The view from the outlook platform running just below the top of the tower is impressive too. In the adjacent Museum of Torture (daily 10–6) you can even listen to a bomb attack, as you huddle in one of the authentic shelters of World War II.

🔲 D6 ⊠ Fritz-Grünbaum-Platz 1 (in Esterhazypark) ☎ 587 14 17 ⏰ Daily 9–6 (Thu until 9) 🍴 Café 🚇 U3 to Neubaugasse 🚌 13A to Esterhazygasse/Haus des Meeres, 57A to Haus des Meeres 🚻 Good 💰 Expensive (viewing platform included)

HOFMOBILIENDEPOT
www.hofmobiliendepot.at

Fascinating collection of furniture made by craftsmen for their Habsburgs patrons from the time of Maria Theresa onward.

🔲 C6 ⊠ Mariahilferstrasse 88 ☎ 524 33 57 ⏰ Tue–Sun 10–6 🍴 Chinese restaurant 🚇 U3 to Zieglergasse 🚻 Good (use entrance on Andreasgasse) 💰 Moderate

KAISERIN ELISABETH DENKMAL

Monument erected following the assassination of the popular empress by an anarchist in Geneva in 1898.

🔲 E4 ⊠ Volksgarten (Burgtheater end) 🚋 Trams 1, 2 to Burgtheater

NASCHMARKT

Here you can sample everything from truffles to oysters at several restaurants among the stalls. The two ends of the market are marked by buildings of the Viennese Jugendstil: at Getreidemarkt to the east is the Secession building by Joseph Olbrich; and at Kettenbrückengasse to the west are two apartment houses with floral ornaments on their façades by Otto Wagner, who also designed the nearby underground station of the U4.

🔲 E6 ⊠ Wienzeile from Getreidemarkt to Kettenbrückengasse ⏰ Mon–Fri 6am–7.30pm, Sat 6–5 🚇 U4 to Kettenbrückengasse

Picasso Triggerfish in Haus des Meeres

Imperial Furniture Depot

NATURHISTORISCHES MUSEUM

www.nhm-wien.ac.at

Historicist architecture and modern display. Dinosaur skeletons and the 25,000-year-old Venus of Willendorf.
➕ E5 ✉ Maria-Theresien-Platz ☎ 521 77-0 🕐 Wed–Mon 9–6.30 (Wed until 9pm). Closed 1 Jan, 1 May, 1 Nov, 25 Dec 🚇 U2 Volkstheater 🚋 Trams 1, 2, D, J Dr-Karl-Lueger-Ring 🚹 Good, use entrance at Burgring 7 🖐 Moderate

PARLAMENT

www.parlament.gv.at

The impressive marble hall and former Imperial Diet are worth seeing on a guided tour. Once the parliament of the western half of the Austro-Hungarian Empire, this was the cradle of politicians from the many nations represented on its benches, including the founder president of the Czechoslovakian Republic, Tomas G. Masaryk, and the Italian Prime Minister Alcide de Gasperi.
➕ D4 ✉ Dr. Karl Renner-Ring 3 ☎ 40 110-2400 🕐 Guided tours: mid-Sep to mid-Jul Mon, Tue, Fri, Sat 11–4; mid-Jul to mid-Sep Mon–Sat 11–4 (except 15 Aug). No tours when Parliament is sitting. Closed public hols 🚇 U2 Volkstheater 🚹 Good 🖐 Inexpensive

THEATER AN DER WIEN

www.theater-wien.at

Original owner Emanuel Schikaneder, librettist for Mozart's *Magic Flute*, complained that he had written 'such a good piece, but Mozart ruined it all with his music'. A shrewd impresario, Schikaneder would have appreciated the theatre's success with such musicals as *Cats*, which ran for 11 years.
➕ E6 ✉ Linke Wienzeile 6 ☎ 588 85 🚇 U1, U2, U4 to Karlsplatz

VOLKSGARTEN

Dominated by the Doric Theseus-Tempel, the Volksgarten is an oasis of tranquillity in the heart of the city.
➕ E4 ✉ Dr-Karl-Renner-Ring 🕐 Daily May–end Sep 6am–10pm; Oct–end Apr 6am–9pm 🚇 U3 to Volkstheater 🚋 Trams 1, 2, D, J to Parlament

Volksgarten

Relaxing with a book in the Volksgarten

Ringstrasse Circle

A walk along Vienna's Ringstrasse, which encircles the historic old city and offers a panorama of Historicist buildings and elegant parks.

DISTANCE: 5km (3.1 miles) **ALLOW:** 3 hours

START

SCHWEDENPLATZ
✚ G3/4 🚇 U1, U4 to Schwedenplatz

END

SCHWEDENPLATZ

① Walk along the Franz-Josefs-Kai westward from Schwedenplatz, then follow the Ring southward. On your right (in Deutschmeisterplatz) is the Rossauer Kaserne (once a barracks).

② Almost immediately to your left is Theophil Hansen's graceful Börse (Stock Exchange). Continue across Schottentor. Set back on your right you will pass the Votivkirche (▷ 71), then the neo-Renaissance university.

③ Continue to the Burgtheater (▷ 51) opposite the Rathaus (City Hall, ▷ 55). Walk on past the Parlament (▷ 58) on your right, while to your left is the Volksgarten (▷ 58).

④ Continuing east on the Ring you reach on your right the Naturhistorisches Museum (▷ 58), the Kunsthistorisches Museum (▷ 52–53) and the monument to Maria Theresa.

⑧ Finally you pass the former War Ministry, and follow the Ring round to its end, leaving the Urania cultural centre on your right and returning to Schwedenplatz on Franz-Josefs-Kai.

⑦ Leave the Stadtpark at the east end near the Museum of Applied Art. Cross the Ringstrasse to Georg-Coch-Platz and walk past Otto Wagner's Austrian Post Office Savings Bank (▷ 34).

⑥ Continuing southeast on the Ring, you will see on your right the Hotel Imperial, then Schwarzenberg-platz. Next enter the Stadtpark (▷ 35) near the Strauss Monument (▷ 35).

⑤ Continue past Schillerplatz, with its statue to the poet Schiller in front of the Academy of Fine Arts, to the State Opera on your left (▷ 35).

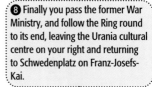

Shopping

HINTERMAYER BÜCHERMARKT

Lots of bargains at this bookshop with some English titles.

🔹 E4 ✉ Herrengasse 5 ☎ 533 79 28 🕐 Mon–Fri 10–6, Sat 10–5 🚇 U3 to Herrengasse

Also at:

🔹 C6 ✉ Neubaugasse 29 and 36 ☎ 523 02 25-13 🕐 Mon–Fri 10–6.15, Sat 10–5 🚇 U3 to Neubaugasse

MODUS VIVENDI

Wide selection of quality knitwear for the whole family, both made-to-measure and off the peg.

🔹 D6 ✉ Schadekgasse 4 ☎ 587 28 23 🕐 Mon–Fri 11–7, Sat 12–5 🚇 U3 to Neubaugasse

NASCHMARKT

Vienna's gourmet market is a must to visit—sample its wares in the many small restaurants.

🔹 E6 ✉ Between the Linke and Rechte Wienzeile 🕐 Permanent market Mon–Fri 6am–7.30pm, Sat 6–5pm. Restaurants to 10pm 🚇 U4 to Kettenbrückengasse

NATURKOST ST. JOSEF

The organic food range here includes items like South American quinoa.

🔹 C6 ✉ Zollergasse 26 ☎ 526 68 18 🕐 Mon–Fri 9–7, Sat 9–4 🚇 U3 to Neubaugasse

RAUMINHALT

An unusual shop devoted to decorative objects and furniture of the last five decades. Plastic is particularly well represented with the 1950s a specialty.

🔹 E7 ✉ Schleifmühlgasse 13 ☎ 409 98 92 🕐 Tue–Fri 12–7, Sat 10–3 🚌 Bus 59A to Schleifmühlgasse. Trams 62, 65, Badner Bahn to Paulanergasse

RINGSTRASSEN-GALERIEN

www.ringstrassen-galerien.at Vienna's elegant, state-of-the-art shopping mall is close to the opera. Here you will find designer brands, a luxury supermarket and gastronomic delicacies from Asayake Sushi to Testa Rossa Coffee Bar.

🔹 F5 ✉ Kärntner Ring 🕐 Shops: Mon–Fri 10–7, Sat 10–6; restaurants: daily 8am–1am 🚇 U1, U2, U4 Karlsplatz 🚋 Trams 1, 2 to Kärntner Ring/Oper

SPITTELBERG MARKET

All through the year local handicrafts are sold in the Spittelberg area in small shops. Before Christmas there is a market in the street replacing the summer gardens of the restaurants.

🔹 D5 ✉ Spittelberggasse 🕐 Mid-Nov to 23 Dec daily 2pm–9pm, Sat–Sun 10–9 🚋 Tram 49 to Stiftgasse

SZÁSZI HÜTE

A traditional hatmakers—one of a dying breed of shop. The service is attentive.

🔹 E6 ✉ Mariahilferstrasse 4 ☎ 522 56 52 🕐 Mon–Wed 10–6, Thu–Fri 10–12.30 🚇 U2 to MuseumsQuartier

VINOTHEK VINISSIMO

Some 400 different Austrian wines can be bought here. Since the 1980s, when it was found that glycol had been added to wines to make them sweeter, Austrian wine has had the strictest product regulations in Europe and its quality is often overlooked.

🔹 D6 ✉ Windmühlgasse 20 ☎ 586 48 88 🕐 Mon–Sat 11–11 🚇 U3 to Neubaugasse

Entertainment and Nightlife

ARNOLD SCHÖNBERG CENTER

Not only a concert hall, but also an archive library and exhibition hall dedicated to the founder of Vienna modernism.

➕ G6 ✉ Schwarzenbergplatz 6 (entrance Zaunergasse 1) ☎ 712 18 88 🕐 Mon–Fri 10–5. Closed hols 🚌 Bus 4A to Lisztrasse or Akademietheater; tram 71 to Am Heumarkt

BURGKINO

This small foreign-language cinema keeps its finger on the pulse.

➕ E5 ✉ Opernring 19 ☎ 587 84 06 🚇 U1, U2, U4 to Karlsplatz/Oper

BURGTHEATER

If you speak German, try to watch a performance here. Otherwise, join a tour to see the Gustav and Ernst Klimt frescos (▷ 51).

➕ E4 ✉ Dr-Karl-Lueger-Ring 2 ☎ 51 444 🚊 Trams 1, 2, D to Burgtheater

FLEX

One of downtown Vienna's best places for DJ music, and still exuding alternative flair.

➕ F2 ✉ At the Danube Canal, downstairs from Augartenbrücke ☎ 533 75 25 🕐 Daily 9pm–4am 🚇 U2, U4 to Schottenring

PAVILLON IM VOLKSGARTEN

A preferred venue in an attractive setting, with an open-air dance floor.

➕ E4 ✉ Burgring 1 ☎ 532 09 07 🕐 May to mid-Sep daily 11am–2am 🚇 U3 to Volkstheater 🚊 Trams 1, 2, D, J to Dr-Karl-Renner-Ring

THEATER AN DER WIEN—DAS NEUE OPERNHAUS

This theatre, where such famous works as Beethoven's *Fidelio* and Strauss's *Die Fledermaus* were first performed, now houses Vienna's 'New Opera House', where lesser known operas and ballets are shown. The artistic standards are high.

OUTRAGE & EXCELLENCE

From 1986 until 1999, the Burgtheater–the flagship of Austrian drama–was under the direction of Claus Peymann, a German whose radical productions and prejudiced political statements were inimical to the Austrian establishment. Resignations ensued when he imported 80 German actors, and although his contract was renewed, his application for Austrian citizenship was turned down. He was known for his challenging and imaginative productions of contemporary drama and the classics, and for nurturing the talent of Thomas Bernhard, Austria's greatest contemporary writer. His successor, after a successful spell at the Volksoper, has adopted a lower profile.

The popular repertoire is left to the Staatsoper and the Volksoper.

➕ E6 ✉ Linke Wienzeile 6 ☎ 588 30-660 🚇 U1, U2, U4 to Karlsplatz (Secession exit)

THEATER IN DER JOSEFSTADT

Once the powerhouse of the famous player-director, Max Reinhardt, who co-founded the Salzburg Festival, this theatre, built in 1788, was renovated in neo-classical style by Joseph Kornhäusel in the 1820s and is especially close to Viennese hearts. Particularly striking are the ornate chandeliers. Outside, plaques honour Reinhardt and Hugo von Hofmannsthal, the latter a leading 20th-century dramatist and the librettist for several operas by Richard Strauss. Jugendstil drama is still played and promoted here constantly.

➕ C4 ✉ Josefstädterstrasse 26 ☎ 42 700 🚊 Tram J to Lederergasse/Strozzigasse

VIENNA'S ENGLISH THEATRE

This theatre presents solid productions of mainstream drama from England and America, given a bit of pep by visiting stars. Thoroughly worthy and occasionally heights-scaling.

➕ D4 ✉ Josefsgasse 12 ☎ 402 12 60 🚇 U2 to Lerchenfelderstrasse 🚊 Tram J to Rathaus

ENTERTAINMENT AND NIGHTLIFE

Restaurants

PRICES

Prices are approximate, based on a 3-course meal for one person.

€€€ over €40
€€   €20–€40
€   under €20

AKAKIKO (€€)

www.akakiko.at
Better value than many Japanese restaurants. The bonus here is the delightful roof terrace.

🚻 D6 ✉ Mariahilferstrasse 40–48 (5th floor of Gerngross store) ☎ 057 333 150
🕐 Daily 10.30–midnight
🚇 U3 to Neubaugasse

ALTE BACKSTUBE (€€)

www.backstube.at
An extremely charming café and restaurant, especially preferred by theatre-goers to the nearby Theater in der Josefstadt (▷ 61). It is in a 300-year-old baroque house with 'Pawlatschen' galleries in the courtyard, and incorporates (as a museum) a bakery formerly on the premises.

🚻 D4 ✉ Lange Gasse 34
☎ 406 11 01 🕐 Tue–Fri 11–midnight, Sat–Sun 12–12
🚇 U2 to Rathaus 🚋 Tram J to Rathaus

CAFÉ LANDTMANN (€€)

www.landtmann.at
One of the classic Ringstrassen cafés, frequented by foreign correspondents reading international newspapers and by local ones attending the frequent press conferences held on its premises. Very political!

🚻 E4 ✉ Dr.-Karl-Lueger-Ring 4 ☎ 24 100-0 🕐 Daily 7.30–midnight. Live piano music Sun–Tue 8pm–11pm; Jul, Aug not Sun 🚋 Trams 1, 2 to Burgtheater

CAFÉ SCHWARZENBERG (€€)

www.cafe-schwarzenberg.at
This is the oldest of the elegant Ringstrassen cafés, opened in 1861 when the boulevard was still under construction. There is a choice of newspapers, including foreign ones, and there are sybaritic touches, like the large selection of cigars for sale.

🚻 G6 ✉ Kärntner Ring 17
☎ 512 8998-13 🕐 Sun–Fri 7am–midnight, Sat 9am–midnight 🚋 Trams 1, 2, D to Schwarzenbergplatz

NEUE WIENER KÜCHE

Nouvelle cuisine arrived late in the city. The man chiefly responsible for its introduction was Werner Matt, a Tyrolean chef who came to the Hilton in the 1970s. As a result, *Selbstmord mit Gabel und Messer* (suicide with a knife and fork) subsided. Menus grew shorter, and the city's kitchens began to use more fresh produce to reduce flour, fat and deep-frozen ingredients.

COBURG (€€€)

www.coburg.at
One of the most successful newcomers to the Vienna restaurant scene. The purist design in historic premises makes this an especially stylish eatery. The glitterati are attracted by the very substantial wine list, perhaps the best in Vienna.

🚻 G5 ✉ Coburgbastei 4
☎ 518 18-800, 518 18-818
🕐 Tue–Sat 6.30pm–midnight. Closed hols 🚇 U3 Stubentor
🚋 Trams 1, 2 to Weihburggasse

EILES (€)

Situated in a mainly residential area, this is a congenial, old-fashioned establishment with window seats and niches. Small menu at midday.

🚻 D4
✉ Josefstädterstrasse 2
☎ 405 3410 🕐 Mon–Fri 7am–10pm, Sat–Sun, hols 8am–10pm 🚋 Tram J to Rathaus

GREEN COTTAGE (€€)

www.greencottage.at
Close to Naschmarkt, this Chinese restaurant is remarkably successful at mingling European and Asiatic styles of cooking in an extremely creative menu. The ingredients (such as fillet of lamb or beef) may seem very Viennese, but the spicy gastronomic experience is made in Sichuan.

🚻 E7 ✉ Kettenbrücken-gasse 3 ☎ 586 6581

🕐 Mon–Sat 11.30–3, 6–11
🚇 U4 to Kettenbrückengasse

HIMMELSSTUBE (€€€)
www.himmelsstube-schickhotels.com
This restaurant on the top floor of the Hotel am Parkring has views over the city's rooftops. Popular for special occasions and intimate dinner rendezvous. There is even a 'Celestial Wedding-Day' offer, which includes wine and a romantic overnight stay at the hotel.
➕ G5 ✉ Hotel Am Parkring, Parkring ☎ 12514 80 417 🕐 Daily 12–2.30, 6–10; Jul, Aug 6pm–10.30pm only 🚇 U3 to Stubentor 🚋 Trams 1, 2 to Weihburggasse

KUPFERDACHL (€€)
www.leupold.at
Well-liked restaurant that keeps up a tradition of authentic Austrian cuisine. Meals are served in rooms decorated with antique weapons and the like.
➕ E3 ✉ Schottengasse 7 ☎ 5339381-0 🕐 Daily 10–midnight 🚇 U2 to Schottentor 🚋 Trams 1, 2, D to Schottentor

PIARISTENKELLER (€€€)
Crammed into the brick vaults of the Piarist monastery, this restaurant is one of the most convivial in Vienna. It is decorated with flags, pictures and historic items. Don't miss the mildly Pythonesque hat

parade, in which you may be invited to participate.
➕ C4 ✉ Piaristengasse 45 ☎ 406 01 93 🕐 Daily 6pm–midnight 🚋 Tram J Lederergasse/Strozzigasse

RATHAUSKELLER (€€)
www.wiener-rathauskeller.at
Located in the huge neo-Gothic Rathaus (City Hall, ▷ 55), the restaurant's various rooms are decorated in Historicist style. It's big enough to escape the bus parties and the food is good.
➕ D4 ✉ New City Hall, Rathausplatz 1/Felderstrasse ☎ 405 12 10 🕐 Mon–Sat 11.30–3, 6–11 🚇 U2 to Rathaus

---

THE *BEISL*

Most restaurants that offer genuine Viennese cooking are carrying on the *Beisl* tradition: honest food, cooked and served in unpretentious surroundings. The word is of Yiddish origin (in the past, tavern keepers were often Jewish). Prosperity, tourism and the profit motive have transformed some *Beisls* into expensive restaurants, but many hold to tradition and keep prices fair. Typical dishes include *Tafelspitz* (boiled beef), *Zwiebelrostbraten* (beefsteak with crispy onions) and *Beuschel* (chopped lung in sauce). Liver is also popular.

SLUKA (€€)
www.sluka.at
Another candidate for the title of Vienna's best, with mouthwatering pastries and light lunches.
➕ D4 ✉ Rathausplatz 8 ☎ 405 7172 🕐 Mon–Fri 8–7, Sat 8–5.30 🚋 Tram J to Rathaus

SMUTNY (€)
www.smutny.com
Despite it's rather suburban or even rustic flair this low cost pub with genuine Viennese kitchen and Czech beer is popular with opera and concert goers. Both the Oper and the Konzerthaus are nearby.
➕ F5 ✉ Elisabethstraße 8 ☎ 587 13 56 🕐 Daily 10 am–midnight 🚇 U1, U2, U4 Karlsplatz 🚋 Trams 1, 2, D, J, 62, 65, Badner Bahn, Buses 3A, 4A, 59A

ZU EBENER ERDE UND ERSTER STOCK (€€)
The Spittelberg area has many good eateries but this is the best. Viennese cooking with a light touch and much attention to seasonal specialties like asparagus. Very good wine list. The posher restaurant part is upstairs, while the lower part is less pretentious; good atmosphere in both.
➕ D5 ✉ Burggasse 13 ☎ 523 62 54 🕐 Mon–Fri 7am–8pm, Sat 6–midnight 🚇 U3 to Volkstheater

Apfelschnitte
€ 2,60

Alsergrund is a residential area dotted with palaces, churches and other places of interest, notably Sigmund Freud's home, where he lived for 47 years.

Around Alsergrund

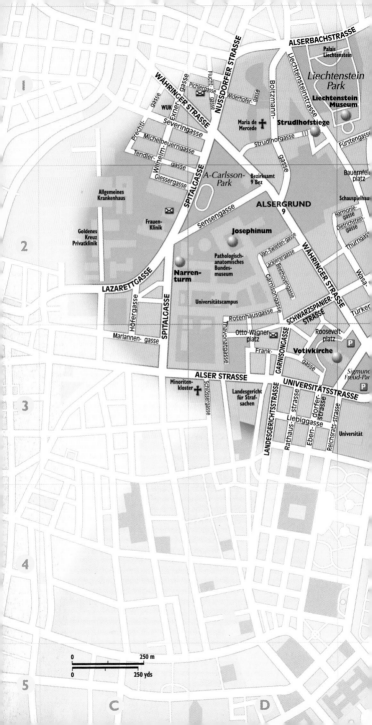

ALSERBACHSTRASSE

Palais
Liechtenstein

Liechtenstein
Park

WÄHRINGER STRASSE

NUSSDORFER STRASSE

Pichlergasse

Flucht-gasse

Exner-gasse

Widerhofer-gasse

Boltzmann-gasse

Liechtensteinstrasse

Liechtenstein
Museum

WUK

Severingasse

Precht-gasse

Michelbeuerngasse

Maria de
Mercede

Strudlhofstiege

Wilhelm-gasse

Tendler-gasse

Glessergasse

SPITALGASSE

strudlhofgasse

Fürstengasse

A-Carlsson-
Park

Bezirksamt
9 Bez

Bauernfeld
platz

Allgemeines
Krankenhaus

Sensengasse

ALSERGRUND
9

Schauspielhaus

Harmonie-gasse

Dietrichstein-gasse

Frauen-
Klinik

Josephinum

Van-Swieten-gasse

Thurnasse

Goldenes
Kreuz
Privatklinik

Lackiergasse

WÄHRINGER STRASSE

Wasa

Narren-
turm

Pathologisch-
anatomisches
Bundes-
museum

Garnisongasse

Türker

LAZARETTGASSE

SPITALGASSE

Höfergasse

Universitätscampus

Rotenhausgasse

SCHWARZSPANIER-
STRASSE

Roosevelt-
platz

P

Mariannen-gasse

Thaviohstrasse

Otto-Wagner-
platz

Frank-

Votivkirche

gasse

Sigmund
Freud-Par

ALSER STRASSE

Minoriten-
kloster

Schlösslgasse

Landesgericht
für Straf-
sachen

GARNISONGASSE

UNIVERSITÄTSSTRASSE

P

LANDESGERICHTSSTRASSE

Rathaus-strasse

Eben-dorfer-strasse

Reichsrats-strasse

Universität

Liebiggasse

0   250 m

0   250 yds

C

D

1

2

3

4

5

Porzellangasse

Glaser-gasse

Roemerlöwengasse

Schulz-

Strassnitzki-gasse

Roger-gasse

Theater-center-Forum

Seegasse

ROSSAUER LÄNDE

Rossauer-Steg

Pramer-

D'Orsay-Gasse

Hahn-gasse

gasse

Rossauer Lände

Grünentor-

P

Müllnergasse

Mosergasse

Servitengasse

gasse

Serviten-gasse

Servitenkirche

Porzellangasse

International Theatre

ROSSAUER-BRÜCKE

Freud Museum

Berggasse

TÜRKENSTRASSE

AUGARTEN-BRÜCKE

Berggasse

FRANZ-JOSEFS-KAI

Donaukanal

Liechtensteinstrasse

strasse

HÖRLGASSE

Schlick-platz

STRASSE

Deutsch-meisterplatz

Ringturm

Franz-Josefs-kai

Schottenring

Gonzagagasse

Zelinka-gasse

gasse

Kolingasse

MARIA-THERESIEN

P

SCHOTTENRING

Börsegasse

Neutorgasse

Schottentor-Universität

Hessgasse

Börse

DR KARL-LUEGER-RING

E

F

Freud Museum

Inside Freud's apartment (left); decorative window (middle); some of Freud's personal effects (right)

THE BASICS

www.freud-museum.at
✚ E2
✉ Berggasse 19
☎ 319 15 96
🕐 Jul–end Sep daily 9–5;
Oct–end Jun 9–6
🚇 U2 to Schottentor
🚊 Tram D to Schlickgasse
♿ None
💰 Moderate

HIGHLIGHTS

● Lecture Hall
● Library
● Research Centre
● Art collection

Some of the 20th century's most influential ideas came from the tenant of No. 5, Berggasse 19. Whether you think of Freud as a genius or as a cantankerous authoritarian, it is interesting to see the place where his work began.

Sigmund Freud Recognized as the founder of modern psychoanalysis, Freud (1856–1939) was nonetheless typically Viennese, playing *tarock* (a card game still popular with the older generation), visiting Café Landtmann (▷ 62) and taking a daily constitutional along the entire length of the Ringstrasse. Like many other gifted Jewish Viennese, Freud opted for medicine, partly because it was a profession in which discrimination was not the barrier that it could be in the army and bureaucracy. He pursued a career at the University of Vienna, where he became an Associate Professor in 1902.

Theories Freud's most controversial theory was that infantile sexual impulses were at the root of adult neuroses. Adler and Jung—the other famous early psychoanalysts—parted company with him over this. However, many now-mainstream concepts started with Freud—for example, division of the personality into id and ego, and the ideas of sublimation and the Oedipus complex. Although many academics still accept Freud's dogmas as axiomatic, his critics believe that he doctored his evidence. The Viennese writer Karl Kraus, a contemporary of Freud's, remarked: 'Psychoanalysis is the disease of which it purports to be the cure'.

Archway (left) in front of the Liechtenstein Museum (right)

★ Liechtenstein Museum
TOP 25

In a superbly renovated palace is displayed a major part of the artistic patrimony of this celebrated family, rulers of the principality of the same name.

The Liechtensteins One of the oldest noble families of Europe, the Liechtensteins were first mentioned in 1136. They derive their name from Liechtenstein Castle, which is a stone's throw from Vienna. Elevated to Princes in 1608, in 1719 they acquired their own sovereign state.

Garden Palace When Hitler invaded Austria in 1938, the Prince of Liechtenstein retreated to his own pocket-handkerchief state, taking his famous art collection with him. In 2004, part of that collection was returned to the family's Garden Palace (summer palace) in Vienna. A state-of-the-art gallery was created to make viewing as pleasurable and informal as possible, so you feel you are enjoying the pictures as the Liechtensteins would themselves have done.

The collection No attempt has been made to stuff the rooms with as much art as possible, and the clear aim is to maximize the viewer's pleasure; if you want to know more there is a helpful audio guide. As the museum's publicity puts it, this is meant to be 'a world of baroque pleasures'–and that's indeed what it has become. To masterpieces ranging from Gothic to *fin de siècle*, it has recently added the Badminton Cabinet, which was originally made for an ancestor of the Duke of Beaufort by Florentine craftsmen in 1732.

THE BASICS

www.liechtenstein museum.at

🚇 E1

✉ Fürstengasse 1

☎ 319 57 67-252

🕐 Sun 10–5 or by appointment

🍽 Restaurants in courtyard

🚌 Bus 40 A, tram D to Bauernfeldplatz, tram 5 to Franz-Josefs-Bahnhof

♿ Good

💰 Expensive, but good discounts, especially for families

❓ Concert included in ticket every Sun 2–3 except Jul, Aug

HIGHLIGHTS

● Badminton Cabinet, the most expensive piece of furniture ever purchased in an auction sale (€27 million in 2004)
● Large series of Rubens paintings
● Baroque garden reconstructed from old prints

Narrenturm

Fools' Tower (left); the Museum of Pathological Anatomy (right) is now housed in the tower

THE BASICS

www.narrenturm.at

✚ C2

✉ Spitalgasse 2, then follow signs to Courtyard 13

☎ 406 86 72-2

🕐 Sep–Jul Wed 3pm–6pm, Thu 8am–11am, first Sat of month 10am–1pm. Closed on hols

Ⓢ Schottentor

🚃 Tram 5 Lazarettgasse; 43, 44 Lange Gasse

♿ None

💷 Inexpensive

❓ Tours by arrangement

HIGHLIGHTS

● 1820s apothecary's shop
● Specimens in formaldehyde
● Abnormal skeletons
● Diseased lungs
● The world's best kidney and gallstone collection

You may find it bizarre or gruesome but you won't forget a visit to this 18th-century, circular Fools' Tower, now home to a museum. Be prepared for its gruesome medical chamber of horrors.

Utopian design The Narrenturm is a strange cylindrical building with a circular inner courtyard divided in half by an extra wing. It was built by Isidore Canevale in 1784 on the orders of Emperor Joseph II, who had also founded the Vienna General Hospital in the same grounds. Each of its five floors had 28 centrally heated cells for mental patients, called fools in the parlance of the day; however, not everyone here was actually mad. The emperor reprimanded one aristocrat, Count Seilern, for shutting his son in here because the young man refused to wed the bride selected for him.

Piece of cake The Viennese have always had an irreverent attitude to the Fools' Tower, calling it the Emperor Joseph's *Gugelhupf* because it is supposed to resemble the locally prized pound cake. Unpopular politicians with ill-thought-out policies are often said to 'belong in the *Gugelhupf*'.

Museum The Narrenturm was used as an asylum until 1866; subsequently it housed a store and provided living quarters for medical staff. It is now the Museum for Pathological Anatomy, and contains a large collection of medical curiosities. After your visit, recover from its horrors by relaxing in one of the students' restaurants in Court 1.

More to See

JOSEPHINUM

Aspiring military surgeons pored over lifelike anatomical wax models here, preparing for a career on the battle-fields of the Empire. Joseph II had seen firsthand the terrible suffering caused by medical ineptitude.

⊞ D2 ⊠ Währinger Strasse 25 ☎ 4277-63422 🕒 Mon–Fri 9–3, first Sat of month 10–2. Closed hols 🚋 Trams 37, 38, 40, 41, 42 to Sensengasse 💷 Inexpensive ❓ Tours on request in advance

SERVITENKIRCHE

The fine cupola of the Servite Church served as a prototype for other baroque churches in the city. A chapel inside is dedicated to the Servite St. Peregrine, who is invoked for healing lameness (Joseph Haydn was among his supplicants). The saint was a great benefactor of the poor, in remembrance of which special bread rolls are distributed in the Servitengassse during the two days of St. Peregrine's fair in May.

⊞ E2 ⊠ Servitengasse 9 ☎ 317 61 95-0 🕒 Daily 8–7 🚇 U4 Rossauer Lände

🚋 Tram D to Schlickgasse 🚶 Two steps 💷 Free

STRUDLHOFSTIEGE

This graceful art nouveau stairway with lanterns and wells was designed in 1910 by Theodor Jäger. The steps are especially attractive at night, when the stairway lanterns throw a soft light on the silvery stone.

⊞ D1 ⊠ Strudlhofgasse 🚇 U4 Rossauer Lände 🚋 Tram D

VOTIVKIRCHE

This huge neo-Gothic church was built to commemorate Franz Josef's escape from an assassination attempt in 1853. Its chapels are dedicated to Austrian regiments. Note the Renaissance sarcophagus of Count Salm, defender of Vienna in the Turkish siege of 1529.

⊞ D3 ⊠ Rooseveltplatz 8 ☎ 406 11 92-0 🕒 Thu–Sat 9–1, 4–6, Sun 9–1. Museum: Tue–Fri 4–6, Sat 10–1 🚇 U2 to Schottentor 🚋 Trams 1, 2 to Schottentor 🚶 Several steps 💷 Church free; museum inexpensive ❓ Holy Mass in English Sun at 11

Josephinum

Strudlhofstiege

Alsergrund Stroll

This is an attractive residential area of Vienna, dotted with a variety of churches, palaces and museums.

DISTANCE: 4km (2.5 miles) **ALLOW:** 2 hours without visits

START

SCHOTTENTOR
✚ E3 🚇 U2 to Schottentor 🚋 Trams 1, 2

END

SCHOTTENTOR

❶ Approach the overblown neo-Gothic Votivkirche (▷ 71) by walking through the Sigmund Freud Park opposite the Schottentor tram junction.

❽ Refreshment is available at several cheaper restaurants here. After leaving the campus by the exit to your left, return to Schottentor on foot or one stop on the tram.

❷ On leaving the church, turn northeast onto Währinger Strasse. Continue to the next traffic lights, then take a right down Berggasse to the Freud Museum (▷ 68).

❼ From the Josephinum, take two right turns for Van-Swieten-Gasse. Once inside the university campus, follow the Leopold-Bauer-Weg to the Narrenturm (▷ 70) screened by trees to your right. Retrace Leopold-Bauer-Weg and continue through Courtyard 7 to Courtyard 1.

❸ Continue along Berggasse until the crossroads, then follow the lively Servitengasse to the Servitenkirche (▷ 71). Good local fare at the Servitenstüberl.

❻ Cross Liechtensteinstrasse and climb the art nouveau steps of Strudlhofstiege (▷ 71). Take Boltzmanngasse to the left and cross Währinger Strasse for the Josephinum (Museum of the History of Medicine, ▷ 71).

❹ From the church turn left and follow Grünentorgasse to the end and turn right on Porzellangasse. A few steps from here turn left for the Liechtenstein Museum (▷ 69) (open on Sunday).

❺ On leaving the palace courtyard, take two right turns.

Shopping

DEMMERS TEEHAUS

www.demmer.at

The genuine Chinese or Indian teas available here will please those who are dispirited by the tea bag and hot water that is sold as 'tea' in cafés and restaurants of notoriously coffee-bound Vienna. Not surprisingly, the founder and owner Andrew Demmer was born in London and returned with his parents from exile after World War II. There is a tea salon upstairs and there are several branches where you can also choose from 250 different types of tea. Trzesniewski's 'unpronouncably good open sandwiches' also belong to Demmer's empire.

➕ E3 ✉ Mölkerbastei 5 ☎ 533 59 95 ⏰ Mon–Fri, 9–6, Sat 9.30–1.30. Tearoom Mon–Fri 10–6 🚇 U2 to Schottentor 🚌 Buses 1A, 3A to Schottentor; trams 1, 2, D to Schottentor

FÜRNIS MÄDCHEN UND BUBEN

www.handpuppen.at

This shop began by importing and selling wooden toys from other countries and factories, but then the owners felt that something was missing. They therefore decided to design toys themselves, creating soft and friendly dolls and animals that are now exported to many countries. Other items

for sale include sleeping bags, bookmarks—and much else.

➕ E2 ✉ Servitengasse 4a ☎ 968 62 33 ⏰ Mon–Fri 9.30–6.30, Sat 9.30–2 🚇 U4 Rossauer Lände 🚊 Tram D Schlickgasse

NÄHZUBEHÖR IRENE HERBERT

If you want to do needlework, or have the patience to sew your own petit-point handbag, this shop provides you with everything you need.

➕ E2 ✉ Servitengasse 6 ☎ 317 71 98 ⏰ Mon–Sat 9–12; Mon, Tue, Thu, Fri also 2–6 🚇 U4 Rossauer Lände 🚊 Tram D Schlickgasse

---

BARGAINS HARD TO FIND

When Austria entered the European Union in 1995, it was expected that prices would fall as a result of more penetration into a previously cartel-ridden and monopolists market. In some areas (chiefly where food is concerned) this has happened, but in luxury goods, prices are oriented to Munich or London and there are no bargains. A tip is to try and buy nonexclusive goods outside the Innere Stadt, where prices are higher because the rents are high and many customers are well-to-do.

TOSTMANN TRACHTEN

www.trostmann.at

This is the place to go for clothing with a *Tracht* (vernacular) look. There are departments for men, woman and children and you may choose between classical and unobtrusive fashion or the full Monty. Every federal province of Austria has its own version of *Tracht*.

➕ E3 ✉ Schottengasse 3A (corner to Mölkerbastei stairs) ☎ 533 53 31 ⏰ Mon–Fri 10–6, Sat 9.30–6 🚇 U2 to Schottentor 🚌 Buses 1A, 3A to Schottentor; trams 1, 2, D to Schottentor

UNGER UND KLEIN

www.ungerundklein.at

The best selection of wines from Lower Austria, Styria and Burgenland. Worth the detour also because of the interior by Eichinger oder Knechtl. They also have a daily wine offer designed to match the weather and your (or their) mood.

➕ F3 ✉ Gölsdorfgasse 2 ☎ 532 13 23 ⏰ Mon–Fri 3–midnight, Sat 5–midnight 🚇 U1, U4 to Schwedenplatz

WERKHAUS

A jumble of tableware, tablecloths, glasses, frames, door bells, lampshades and more.

➕ E2 ✉ Servitengasse 8 ☎ 31 01 573 ⏰ Mon–Fri 3–6, Tue–Sat 10–1 🚇 U4 Rossauer Lände 🚊 Tram D Schlickgasse

AROUND ALSERGRUND

SHOPPING

Entertainment and Nightlife

INTERNATIONAL THEATRE

www.internationaltheatre.at
An enthusiastic company plays to an enthusiastic audience in two rooms, the second, (larger) one being The Fundus housed in a cellar of the nearby Servite Church. Like its older brother, Vienna's English Theatre (▷ 61), the International Theatre serves both Vienna's international community, the locals who like to practise their English and language learners young and old. A fixed point in the annual repertory is Dickens' *A Christmas Carol*, performed in The Fundus in late November and December.

➕ E2 ✉ Porzellangasse 8 (The Fundus: Müllnergasse 6A) ☎ 319 62 72 🚋 Tram D to Schlickgasse

PFARRKIRCHE LICHTENTAL

www.schubertkirche.at
Composer Franz Schubert was the greatest son of the Lichtental parish. The church where he was baptized, received his first exposure to music and where some of his great masses were first performed, has hardly changed from his time. There are Schubert Days in late November and regular organ recitals at other times of the year.

➕ Off map at D1 ✉ Marktgasse 40/Lichtentalergasse ☎ 315 26 46 🚋 Tram D to Althanstrasse

SUMMER STAGE

www.summerstage.co.at
From May to September Vienna's trendy Summer Stage along the Alsergrund Danube Canal is a magnet for young people. Viennese food and international fare is on offer, together with concerts and lectures, exhibitions, sporting facilities—and even a doggy watering hole with all canine comforts.

➕ F1/2 ✉ Rossauer Lände south of Mosergasse ☎ 319 66 44-10 🕐 Daily 5pm–1am, Sun from 3pm 🚇 U4 to Rossauer Lände

VOLKSOPER

www.volksoper.at
Even though it's in the uncongenial area of the *Gürtel* (Ring Road), the Volksoper is no poor relation of the Staatsoper. For visitors this is the best place to enjoy the operettas and some German operas hardly

WELL-KEPT SECRETS

Geheimtips—things that the initiates prefer to keep to themselves—are by definition inclined to be ephemeral. This page describes what might be called perennial *Geheimtips*—places that have established themselves as having something special to offer. They give a taste of the Vienna beyond the superficial glitter it so willingly displays for tourists.

performed in the English-speaking world. For the locals it's a good place to see imported musicals and foreign-language operas in German. There are also ballet and solo performances of entertainers, occasionally one staged by the director himself. The Volksoper may not have the budget to engage internationally acclaimed opera stars, but like the English National Opera or the New York City Opera, it contributes something uniquely democratic to the city's musical scene. Needless to say the tickets also cost less.

➕ C1 ✉ Währinger Strasse 78 ☎ 51 444 🚇 U6 to Währinger Strasse-Volksoper 🚋 Trams 40, 41 42 to Währinger Strasse-Volksoper

WUK

Arts area with café and restaurant, and also performance art, dance and DJ nights. Situated since 1981 in a rundown former locomotive factory, the WUK has developed into one of Europe's largest and hottest art scenes hosting 130 groups. The heart of Vienna's alternative culture, it focuses both on international trends and local innovations.

➕ C1 ✉ Währinger Strasse 59 ☎ 401 210 🕐 Times vary, phone for details 🚇 U6 to Währinger Strasse-Volksoper 🚋 Trams 40, 41, 42 to Währinger Strasse-Volksoper

Restaurants

PRICES

Prices are approximate, based on a 3-course meal for one person.

€€€ over €40
€€ €20–€40
€ under €20

BERG (€€)

www.cafe-berg.at
A long established café and restaurant for the gay community. Adjacent is the Löwenherz (Lionheart) bookshop with gay and feminist literature. Cool atmosphere in a modern setting; well known for its sumptuous brunch (daily 10–3) and constantly changing menu.
🚌 E2 ✉ Berggasse 8/Wasagasse ☎ 319 57 20 🕐 Daily 10am–1am 🚇 U2 Schottentor 🚋 Trams 37, 38, 40, 41, 44 to Berggasse

COUSCOUS (€€)

www.couscous.at
Round the corner from the Servitenkirche. Ideal if you long for food from Egypt and other regions of North Africa. There is a Bedouin corner and you can even smoke a water pipe with natural or apple tobacco.
🚌 E2 ✉ Grünentorgasse 19 ☎ 310 85 17 🕐 Kitchen 12.30pm–10pm 🚋 Tram D Schlickgasse or Bauernfeldplatz

RAGUSA (€€€)

www.ragusa.at
A seafood restaurant with fresh fish flown in daily from the Dalmatian coast

of the Adriatic Sea. Full range of wines from Croatia. Italian cuisine also on offer.
🚌 E2 ✉ Berggasse 15 ☎ 317 15 77 🕐 Mon–Sat 11–3, 6–midnight 🚇 U2 to Schottentor 🚋 Trams 37, 38, 40, 41, 44 to Berggasse

REBHUHN (€€)

A place for a quick lunch at reasonable prices just across from the Freud Museum (▷ 68). Slightly modernized rustic setting where artists, students and the local residents hang out.
🚌 E2 ✉ Berggasse 24/Schlickgasse 🕐 Mon–Fri 11am–midnight, Sat–Sun 5pm–midnight 🚋 Tram D to Schlickgasse

NO-FRILLS FOOD

Cynics say that the preferred dish of a Viennese is a big one. The new self-service restaurants, however, offer much more flexibility in terms of portion size and in range of food (although the cuisine remains Austrian). Vienna's many historic wine vaults also offer local wines and modestly priced food in a convivial and romantic setting. (A 15th-century writer remarked that more of Vienna was below ground than above it.) Sandwich bars offer open-sandwiches, a specialty here, and markets always have stands selling snacks and delicacies.

ROTH (€€)

www.kremslehnerhotels.at
A stylish restaurant offering Viennese classics such as *Tafelspitz* (boiled beef) and *Zwiebelrostbraten* (beef steak with crispy onions). Under the same management as the adjacent Hotel Regina—you can peek from the arcade into the latter's ornate and majestic former dining room.
🚌 E3 ✉ Währinger Strasse 1/Rooseveltplatz ☎ 402 79 95 🕐 Daily 11–midnight 🚇 U2 to Schottentor

SAFRAN (€€€)

www.safran-vienna.at
If the need for a curry overwhelms you, this dignified restaurant with a wide range of Indian specialties will suit.
🚌 D3 ✉ Garnisongasse 10 ☎ 407 42 34 🕐 Daily 11.30–3, 6–11.30 🚋 Trams 40, 41, 42 from Schottentor to Schwarzspanierstrasse

SERVITENSTÜBERL (€€)

www.servitenstueberl.at
Full range of genuine Viennese kitchen in traditional, unpretentious setting. They sell their own wine from Lower Austria.
🚌 E2 ✉ Servitengasse 7 besides Servite Church ☎ 317 55 36 🕐 Kitchen open Tue–Sat 11–3, 6–10; Sun 11–3. Closed last week of Oct and first two weeks in Jan 🚋 Tram D to Schlickgasse ❓ Summer garden

This area features two of Europe's greatest baroque buildings: the Belvedere Palace and Karlskirche. The monumental architecture of both palace and church have justly made the city renowned for its splendid late-flowering of the style.

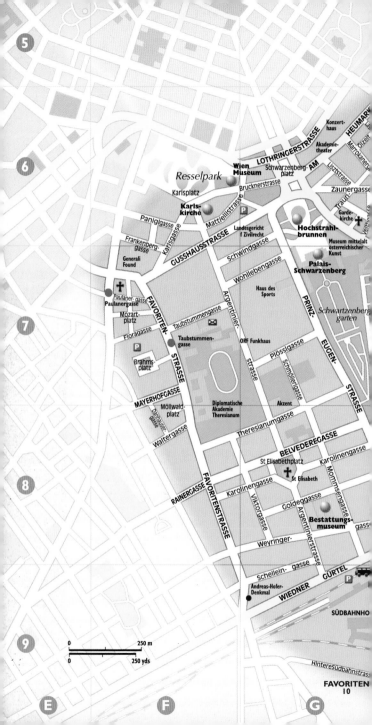

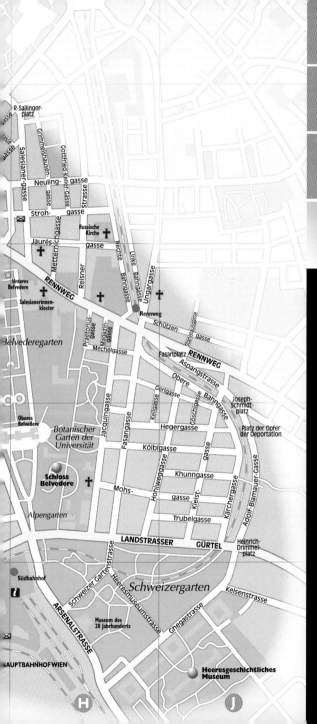

R-Sallinger-platz

Salesianer-gasse

Grimmelshausen-gasse

Gottfried-Keller-gasse

Neuling-gasse

strasse

Stroh-gasse

gasse

Jaurés-gasse

Metternichgasse

Reisner-gasse

Russische Kirche ✝

gasse

Linke Bahngasse

Rechte Bahngasse

Ungargasse

Unteres Belvedere

RENNWEG

Salesianerinnen-kloster

✝

✝

Rennweg

Schützen-gasse

Strohgasse

Stanislausgasse

Belvederegarten

Praetoriusgasse

Magazingasse

Mechelgasse

Fasanplatz

Aspangstrasse

RENNWEG

Obere Bahngasse

Joseph-Schmidt-platz

Oberes Belvedere

Botanischer Garten der Universität

Jacquingasse

Fasangasse

Gerlgasse

Kellgasse

Döschgasse

Hegergasse

Platz der Opfer der Deportation

Schloss Belvedere ✝

Kölblgasse

gasse

Adolf-Blamauer-Gasse

Khunngasse

Kärchergasse

Kleiststrasse

Mohs-gasse

Hohlweggasse

Alpengarten

Trubelgasse

LANDSTRASSER GÜRTEL

Heinrich-Drimmel-platz

Südbahnhof

ℹ

Schweizer Gartenstrasse

Heeresmuseumstrasse

Schweizergarten

Kelsenstrasse

ARSENALSTRASSE

Museum des 20 Jahrhunderts

Chegastrasse

HAUPTBAHNHOF WIEN

Heeresgeschichtliches Museum

H

J

Heeresgeschichtliches Museum

TOP **25**

The beautiful setting of the Museum of Military History (left); the car in which Franz Ferdinand was killed (right)

THE BASICS

www.hgm.or.at
➕ J9
✉ Arsenal, Ghegastrasse
☎ 795 61-603 70
🕐 Sat–Thu 9–5. Closed 1 Jan, Easter Sun, 1 May, 1 Nov, 24, 25, 31 Dec
🍴 Café
🚌 Bus 13A to Südbahnhof; trams O, D, 18 to Südbahnhof
🚆 Schnellbahn to Südbahnhof
♿ Good
💶 Moderate
❓ Audio guide

HIGHLIGHTS

● Ornate Byzantine façade
First floor
● Turkish tent
Ground floor
● *To the Unknown Soldier* (1916), Albin Egger Lienz
● Car in which Archduke Franz Ferdinand was assassinated
● Bloodstained uniform of Archduke Franz Ferdinand
● Tank park

The huge military complex known as the Arsenal and Museum of Military History is notable for its exotic pseudo-Byzantine architecture and for the collection inside, which provides visitors with a fascinating insight into Vienna's imperial history.

Riotproof After the revolution of 1848, during which Am Hof, the old town armoury, was plundered, leading Ringstrassen architects were commissioned to design a riot-proof arms factory and depot. This state-of-the-art complex was built with eight fortress-like barracks along its perimeter; by 1854 the facilities it enclosed were like those of an entire city within a city. The task of constructing it created jobs at a time of social unrest and unemployment. After World War II, part of the complex was rebuilt, and part is now occupied by state-owned drama workshops and the central telephone exchange, as well as the Museum of Military History.

Collection Themed sections include the Thirty Years War (1618–48), the Napoleonic Wars and the Austrian Navy (in existence until 1918). Particularly gruesome is the bloodstained tunic Archduke Franz Ferdinand, heir to the Habsburg throne, was assassinated in—this event triggered the start of World War I. The museum has been redesigned in recent years and now includes a display on 'Republic and Dictatorship' covering the period from the fall of the Habsburg Empire up to 1945.

St. Charles's Church at night (left); column symbolizing the Pillars of Hercules (middle); an angel statue (right)

Karlskirche

AROUND LANDSTRASSE, WIEDEN ★ TOP 25

St. Charles's Church is one of Europe's finest baroque buildings. The symbolism in the two exotic columns at the front, fashioned on Trajan's Column in Rome, illustrates Habsburg secular power and spiritual legitimacy.

Origins In 1713 Vienna was hit by the last of many plagues; Emperor Charles VI vowed to dedicate a church to St. Charles Borromeo, who succoured the people during the 1576 Milan plague. Begun in 1716, it is the masterpiece of Johann Bernhard Fischer von Erlach, who died in 1723 leaving his son, Joseph Emanuel, to complete it in 1739.

Paean in stone The two columns at the front symbolize the Pillars of Hercules in the Mediterranean, a reference to the Spanish realm (by then lost) of the other Habsburg line. Their spiralling friezes show the life of Charles Borromeo. The columns are also emblems of the Emperor's motto, '*Constantia et fortitudine*'). The russet, gold and white interior creates a harmonious tranquillity.

Paintings Austrian and Central European baroque is characterized by bright frescos with transcendental motifs and the Karlskirche houses one of the most splendid examples. Johann Michael Rottmayrs's painting soaring into the cupola shows the *Apotheosis of Charles Borromeo*. Among the other works is *Assumption of the Virgin* by Sebastiano Ricci.

THE BASICS

www.karlskirche.at
✚ F6
✉ Karlsplatz
☎ 504 61 87
🕐 Mon–Sat 9–6, Sun 12–5.45
🚇 U1, U2, U4 to Karlsplatz
🚌 Bus 4A; trams 62, 65 to Karlsplatz
♿ Good
💶 Moderate (cupola and Museo Borromeo included)
❓ Audio guide

HIGHLIGHTS

● *Apotheosis of Charles Borromeo*, J. M. Rottmayr
● *Christ and the Centurion*, Daniel Gran
● *The Healing of the Man with the Palsy*, Giovanni Pellegrini
● Carved pulpit with rocaille and floral decoration

TIP

● It is possible to access the cupola to view the ceiling fresco close up and get a panoramic view of the city.

Schloss Belvedere

TOP
25

AROUND LANDSTRASSE, WIEDEN   TOP 25

HIGHLIGHTS

Lower Belvedere
● B. Permoser's statue of
Prince Eugene
Upper Belvedere
● Sala Terrena with Hercules
figures
● *The Kiss*, Gustav Klimt
● *Death and the Maiden*,
Egon Schiele

TIP

● Visit the fragrant Alpine
Garden adjacent to the
gardens south of the Upper
Belvedere.

**After St. Stephen's Cathedral (▷ 31), the
restored Belvedere Palace is Vienna's
most important landmark. It was built in
the early 18th century for Prince Eugene
of Savoy, the most successful general in
Austria's history.**

Origins Lukas von Hildebrandt constructed the
Lower Belvedere (Unteres Belvedere) between
1714 and 1716. The magnificent Upper
Belvedere (Oberes Belvedere), designed to
house the prince's fabulous art collection, was
built between 1721 and 1723.

Palace in history Emperor Josef II installed the
Imperial Picture Gallery in the Upper Belvedere.
Franz Ferdinand, the heir to the throne, lived here
from 1894 until his assassination in 1914. In

Grand staircase in the palace of the Upper Belvedere; statue of Atlas by Lorenzo Mattielli; the Lower Belvedere; view of the Upper Belvedere over the lake; The Judgement of Paris by Max Klinger (clockwise from far left)

1955 the Austrian State Treaty ending the Allied occupation was signed in the Marble Hall.

Museums The Belvedere galleries underwent complete restructuring in 2007. The main entrance is now at the Lower Belvedere, which contains Prince Eugene's rooms, including the Golden Salon. The adjacent Orangery has been adapted for special exhibitions and the former stables display minor works of medieval art. Major medieval works and baroque paintings are now concentrated in the Upper Belvedere. However the main attraction remains the splendid collection of masterpieces by Klimt, Schiele and Kokoschka, together with international art from the 19th century and later. In 2009 post-1945 art and the Fritz Wotruba collection will be shown at a pavilion in nearby Schweizergarten.

THE BASICS

www.belvedere.at

✚ H8

✉ Lower Belvedere: Rennweg 6; Upper Belvedere: Prinz-Eugen-Strasse 27

☎ 79 557 0

🕐 Collections: daily 10–6 (Wed until 9). Stables: 10–noon. Shorter hours on 1 Jan, 24, 31 Dec. Alpine Garden: Apr–Jul 10–6

🍽 Café in Upper Belvedere

🚋 Tram 71 (Lower Belvedere) and D (Upper Belvedere)

💰 Expensive

♿ Good

❓ Audio guide. Online ticket service

Wien Museum

TOP 25

Entrance to the Wien Museum (left); Lady in a Yellow Dress by Max Kurzweil (right)

THE BASICS

www.wienmuseum.at

➕ F6

✉ Karlsplatz

☎ 505 87 47

🕐 Tue–Sun 9–6. Closed 1 Jan, 1 May, 24 Dec from 2pm, 25 Dec

🍴 Café

🚇 U1, U2, U4 to Karlsplatz

🚌 Bus 4A; tram 62, 65 to Karlsplatz

♿ Good

💶 Moderate. Permanent exhibition free on Sun

HIGHLIGHTS

● Eduard Fischer's maquette of the old town, 1854
● Franz Xaver Messerschmidt's grotesque busts
● *Stephansplatz* (1834), Rudolf von Alt
● Reconstructed apartment of playwright Franz Grillparzer
● Reconstructed sitting room in architect Adolf Loos's house
● *Anna Moll, Writing*, Carl Moll

Although housed in a drab 1950s-style building, the Viennese History Museum is one of Europe's best city museums, and its well-displayed contents bring the Viennese past vividly to life.

Origins The characterless design of the structure—its banality made more striking by its juxtaposition with the baroque architecture of St. Charles's Church next door—aroused considerable anger among Viennese patriots, although it had its defenders.

Museum collection Vienna's history, topography, art and culture are explored in the many works of art and architectural relics, and in the early city plans, reconstructions of interiors like Adolf Loos's living room and Franz Grillparzer's Biedermeier apartment, and beautifully made period models of the city.

Sweeping view The ground floor spans pre-history (Hallstatt culture) up to and including medieval times. On the first floor are exhibits of the baroque period and Enlightenment. The material relating to the time of the Turkish siege (weapons and a portrait of Turkish commander Kara Mustafa) of Vienna is especially interesting. The second floor covers the Congress of Vienna (1814–15), the Biedermeier era (1815–48), the revolution of 1848 and Vienna at the beginning of the 20th century, with examples of the art, artefacts and designs of the Secession (▷ 56), and the later Austrian Expressionism movement.

More to See

BESTATTUNGSMUSEUM

In this Burial Museum, devoted to the undertaker's art, exhibits include photographs of dressed corpses seated on chairs, a stiletto for stabbing the dead through the heart to ensure against being buried alive and a coffin bell-pull for use in such an emergency.

➕ G8 ✉ Goldeggasse 19 ☎ 5019 54227 🕐 By appointment Mon–Fri 12–3 🚊 Tram D to Upper Belvedere 💰 Moderate

HOCHSTRAHLBRUNNEN

In front of the elegant Schwarzenberg Palace at the southern end of Schwarzenbergplatz a huge fountain was erected in 1873 to mark the opening of Vienna's first water supply from the Alpine peaks (*Hochquellen-leitung*). It brought fresh water to the city over a distance of 90km (56 miles). Since 1906, the fountain has been illuminated with tinted lights after nightfall.

➕ G6 ✉ Schwarzenbergplatz 🚊 Trams D to Gusshausstrasse, 71 to Am Heumarkt

PALAIS-SCHWARZENBERG

www.palais-schwarzenberg.com
In 1716, Prince Schwarzenberg bought an unfinished palace by Lukas von Hildebrandt and then commissioned Johann Bernhard Fischer von Erlach, and later his son Josef Emanuel, to complete what is now one of Vienna's best hotels (▷ 112); it is still owned by the family. The grand sweep up to the portico was conceived by the younger Fischer, who also installed Vienna's first steam-driven motor to pump water for the fountains. The Schwarzenbergs' neighbour and rival, Prince Eugene of Savoy, had to postpone his great Schloss Belvedere project (▷ 82–83) until he had persuaded the Schwarzenbergs to sell a vital piece of adjacent land.

➕ G7 ✉ Schwarzenbergplatz 9 ☎ Hotel/restaurant: 798 45 15-0 🕐 Hotel/ restaurant to reopen in 2009. No access to palace and garden 🚊 Tram D to Gusshausstrasse

Bestattungsmuseum

Baroque at its Best

Karlskirche and the Belvedere Palace, with its gardens and fine collection of Secessionist art, are the highlights of this walk.

DISTANCE: 4km (2.5 miles)   **ALLOW:** 2 hours without visits

START

KARLSPLATZ
➕ F6 🚇 U1, U2, U4 to Karlsplatz

END

SÜDBAHNHOF
➕ H9 🚈 S-Bahn; bus 13A; trams D, O, 18

① From the underground passage connecting the Opera and Karlsplatz, take the Resselpark exit to the south. On your left you will see the Karlsplatz pavilions designed by Otto Wagner, while ahead rises Karlskirche (▷ 81).

② On leaving the church, turn south into Argentinierstrasse. At the second crossroads turn left and approach Schwarzenbergplatz through Gusshausstrasse.

③ Cross Prinz-Eugen-Strasse to the Hochstrahlbrunnen (▷ 85) and the Russian Liberation Monument. Bear right into Rennweg with a detour to view the façade of the Palais-Schwarzenberg (▷ 85).

④ Then continue up Rennweg to the entrance of the Belvedere Palace (▷ 82) and museums. Having viewed the Lower Belvedere, walk up the sloping gardens to the Upper Belvedere.

⑧ On leaving the museum through the main gate, turn left into Ghegastrasse and then right into Arsenalstrasse.

⑦ Take the path to the left of the ornamental pool and continue along the promenade. After refreshment in the Schweizergarten restaurant, head up Heeresmuseum Strasse to visit to the Heeresgeschichtliches Museum (▷ 80).

⑥ On leaving the Belvedere, bear right round the building and head for the Alpine Garden to your left. After visiting the latter, retrace your steps through the Belvedere's southern garden as far as the Gürtel (Ring Road), which you cross to reach the Schweizergarten.

⑤ Visit the Upper Belvedere with its collections of art, and enjoy the view of Vienna from the upper windows.

WALK

AROUND LANDSTRASSE, WIEDEN

Shopping

ALOIS FRIMMEL
www.knopfkoenig.at
This shop, founded in 1844, sells only buttons. Maybe the 'old king of buttons' has precisely the one you have been trying to find for years.

🏠 F7 ✉ Zum alten Knopfkönig, Wiedner Hauptstrasse 34
🕐 Mon–Wed 10–4.45, 5.15–6; Fri 10–3.45, 4.15–6; Sat 10–1
🚋 Trams 62, 65, Badner Bahn to Paulanergasse

BACKHAUSEN
www.backhausen.at
The inheritor of the Secession tradition has an extensive range of Wiener Werkstätte, along with Liberty patterns (patterns of the English Arts and Crafts Movement sold by Liberty of London). Considered by many as Vienna's best home furnishing store.

🏠 G5 ✉ Schwarzenbergstrasse 10 ☎ 514 04-0
🕐 Mon–Fri 9.30–6.30, Sat 9.30–5 🚋 Trams 1, 2, 70, D to Schwarzenbergplatz

BADER & PARTNER
www.bader-partner.at
Another rarity shop focusing on balloons and all kinds of display and party products.

🏠 F7 ✉ Wiedner Hauptstrasse 36 ☎ 202 66 60-0 🕐 Mon–Fri 9–6.30
🚋 Trams 62, 65, Badner Bahn to Mayerhofgasse

CASETTA-PAJOR
Good women's suits, plus a large selection of accessories for sale.

🏠 H6 ✉ Landstrasser Hauptstrasse 1B ☎ 713 5118
🕐 Mon–Fri 9–6, Sat 9–5
🚇 U3 to Wien Mitte/ Landstrasse Hauptstrasse

EDI-BÄR
www.edibaer.at
Margit Edinger sells and restores teddy bears, as well as other soft toys. There are home-made bracelets and typically Viennese petit-point bags.

🏠 J5 ✉ Landstrasser Hauptstrasse 28 ☎ 710 25 84 Tue–Fri 10–3, 2–6, Sat 10–1
🚇 U3 Rochusgasse 🚋 Tram O Sechskrügelgasse

LUDWIG REITER
www.ludwigreiter.at
Founded in 1885, this shoemaker maintains a Viennese tradition of solid and comfortable shoes of the finest quality. Reiter has developed a wide

---

TRACHTENMODE
The basis of traditional Austrian dress is peasant and hunting costume. Women wear *Dirndls*—dresses with full skirts and lace blouses that have a tight, revealing bodice—perhaps topped by a stylishly cut velvet jacket. Men wear green cloth jackets with braided cuffs and lapels, sometimes with buttons made from antlers. With its rural origins, and rather showy Austrianness *Trachtenmode* has definite right-wing associations.

---

range of casual shoes, fine leather goods and other accessories. The shop's exclusivity is reflected both in the price and quality of the merchandise.

🏠 F7 ✉ Wiedner Hauptstrasse 41/Schlüsselgasse
☎ 505 82 58 🕐 Mon–Fri 9.30–6, Sat 9.30–5. Closed Sat in Jul, Aug 🚋 Trams 62, 65, Badner Bahn to Mayerhofgasse

MARIOL
www.mariol.at
In this shop women can measure up for 'chic from size 42 upwards', which means appealing clothes for those whose figures won't make the catwalk. You are welcome to make appointments outside the ordinary opening times. It's a place that sells personal style as much as clothes.

🏠 J5 ✉ Landstrasser Hauptstrasse 28 🕐 Mon–Fri 10–6, Sat 10–3, Outlet Tue 10–6 🚇 U3 to Rochusgasse
🚌 Bus 4A to Rochusgasse; tram O to Sechskrügelgasse

PISCHINGER
The eponymous chocolatier offers his own products, one of which is a Viennese classic, the Pischinger Eck—a triangular dark chocolate with the original Pischinger nut-croquant-filling.

🏠 H5 ✉ Landstrasser Hauptstrasse 2C 🕐 Daily 9–6.30 🚇 U3, U4 to Landstrasse 🚋 Tram O to Landstrasse

Entertainment and Nightlife

ARNOLD SCHOENBERG CENTER
www.schoenberg.at
Not only a concert hall, but also an archive library and exhibition hall dedicated to the founder of Viennese modernism.
🞧 G6 ✉ Schwarzenbergplatz 6 ☎ 712 18 88 🚊 Trams D, 1, 2, 71 to Schwarzenbergplatz

BÖSENDORFER SAAL
www.boesendorfer.at
Not to be confused with the once famous Bösendorfersaal in the Inner City, this is a newly adapted auditorium in the headquarters of Vienna's most celebrated pianomaker. Concerts are given by students of a private conservatory, but there are also occasional performances of renowned artists.
🞧 F8 ✉ Graf-Starhemberg-Gasse 14 ☎ 504 66 51 🚇 U1 to Taubstummengasse 🚊 Trams 62, 65 Badner Bahn to Mayerhofgasse

KONZERTHAUS
www.konzerthaus.at
Opened in 1913, the building contains three concert halls: the Grosser Saal, for orchestral performances; and the Mozartsaal and the Schubertsaal for chamber music, modern music and *Lieder* evenings. In summer there are twice-weekly selections of Mozart's music, played by musicians dressed

in period costume.
🞧 G6 ✉ Lothringerstrasse 20 ☎ 242 002 🚇 U4 to Stadtpark

MUSIKVEREIN
www.musikverein.at
The Musikverein is famous for its superb acoustics and sumptuous gilded interior. The Wiener Philharmoniker's New Year's Day Concert is broadcast from here and the orchestra's Sunday concerts are a Viennese institution. During the week there are orchestral concerts in the Great Hall, and chamber music in the Brahmssaal.
🞧 F6 ✉ Bösendorferstrasse 12 ☎ 505 81 90 🚇 U1, U2, U4 to Karlsplatz

---

MUSICAL TASTE

The Musikverein—the concert hall for the Society of the Friends of Music—was founded in the 19th century. Mainstream Viennese taste is conservative: 'The popularity of Brahms', wrote one critic, 'is due largely to his music being exactly suited to Viennese tastes, not too hot and not too cold; it eschews excitement and seldom commits the unforgivable sin of being boring'. But there has always been a radical element. The greatest scandal in the Musikverein's history occurred in 1913 when pro- and anti-modernists began fighting at a Schönberg concert.

PALACES
The city's summer music festival, Wiener Musik-Sommer, offers graceful chamber music in some lovely baroque palaces, among them Palffy, Auersperg and Schwarzenberg.

RADIOKULTURHAUS
www.radiokulturhaus.orf.at
All kinds of music, often in virtuoso performances, may be heard in the Austrian Broadcasting Company's (ORF) Broadcasting Hall or in the adjacent Kulturcafé.
🞧 F7 ✉ Argentinierstrasse 30a ☎ 501 70 377 🚇 U1 to Taubstummengasse

THERESIANUM
www.wieneroperetten sommer.at
A new tradition of Best-of-Operetta revues has been established at the historic open-air stage in the garden of another former summer palace of the Habsburgs.
🞧 F7 ✉ Favoritenstrasse 15 ☎ 505 35 26-0 🚇 U1 to Taubstummengasse

URANIA
Max Fabiani's interesting late Jugendstil building, built between 1904 and 1912, on the Danube Canal was restored a few years ago. A multicultural performance hall.
🞧 H4 ✉ Uraniastrasse 1 ☎ 712 6191-94 🚇 U1, U4 to Schwedenplatz

Restaurants

BODEGA ESPAÑOLA (€)

A taste of Spain in the heart of Vienna's 4th district. Tapas like *pinchos de pollo con arroz* (skewers of grilled chicken on rice) to wash down with a good choice of Spanish wines.

🚇 G8 ✉ Belvedergasse 10 ☎ 504 55 00 🕐 Mon–Sat 6pm–1am 🚊 Tram D to Schloss Belvedere

CASA ALBERTO (€)

An Italian restaurant popular with journalists from the nearby ORF (Austrian Broadcasting Company). Antonio Vivaldi, who would have appreciated the restaurant's Italian cooking, died in a house nearby.

🚇 F7 ✉ Argentinierstrasse 15 ☎ 505 71 76 🕐 Daily 11am–midnight 🚇 U1 to Taubstummengasse 🚊 Tram D to Gusshausstrasse

IM PALAIS SCHWARZENBERG (€€€)

The view of the gardens of the palace is splendid. So is the food. Try the stuffed guinea fowl in white port sauce or the medallions of venison.

Restaurant to reopen in 2009.

🚇 G7 ✉ Schwarzenbergplatz 9 ☎ 798 4515/600 🚊 Tram D to Gusshausstrasse, tram 71 to Am Heumarkt

SALM BRÄU (€)

Bustling beer cellar in a former monastery. Good-value hot and cold food and great beer, some brewed on the premises.

🚇 H7 ✉ Rennweg 8 ☎ 799 59 92 🕐 Daily 11–11 🚊 Tram 71 to Unteres Belvedere

SPERL (€€)

www.restaurant-sperl.at
A reliable restaurant offering a first-class selection of Viennese food. Specialties are the beef classics, such as roasted sirloin with onions (*Wiener Rostbraten*). For dessert, try the *Powidltascherl*, Czech-style dumplings filled with plum compôte, now hard

to get even in Prague. The intimate garden is a romantic place to go in summer.

🚇 G8 ✉ Karolinengasse 13/Mommsengasse ☎ 504 73 34 🕐 Mon–Thu 11–10.30, Fri–Sun 11–10. Closed 2 weeks after Christmas 🚌 Bus 13A; tram D to Schloss Belvedere

STEIRERECK IM STADTPARK (€€€)

www.steirereck.at
A distinguished restaurant in stunning new premises famous for the delicacy of its *Neue Wiener Küche* and its well-chosen wine list. Reserve in advance.

🚇 H5 ✉ Am Heumarkt 2 ☎ 713 31 68 🕐 Mon–Fri 9am–10pm, Sat–Sun 9–7. Closed hols 🚇 U3 to Stubentor or Landstrasse, U4 to Stadtpark (park exit)

ZUR KLEINEN STEIERMARK (€)

A relaxing informal hostelry offering specialties from the province of Styria. Try the *Mistfuhre* (literally: 'a load of rubbish'), which consists of grilled and fried meat with vegetables. In summer the garden with adjacent playground is ideal for a family outing.

🚇 H9 ✉ Heeresmuseumstrasse 1 (in the Schweizergarten) ☎ 799 58 83 🕐 Daily 11–11 (winter Sun 11–10); 25, 26 Dec 11–3. Closed 24 Dec and about 2 weeks after Christmas 🚊 Trams O, 18 to Fasangasse, D to Südbahnhof

Vienna's suburbs were once homeground both for the nobility and for craftsmen, with residential areas, cemeteries and workshops. Just beyond them lies the varied landscape of the Wienerwald and the water meadows of the Danube's flood plain.

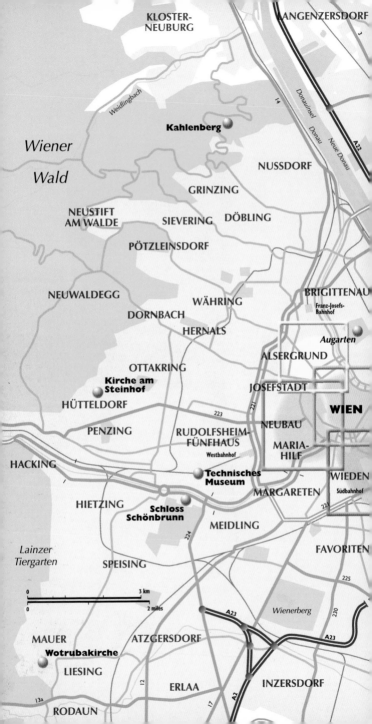

GERASDORF
BEI WIEN

STREBERSDORF

GROSS-
JEDLERSDORF

NEUSÜSSENBRUNN

FLORIDSDORF

LEOPOLDAU

BREITENLEE

KAGRAN

DONAUSTADT

HIRSCH-
STETTEN

Alte Donau

Gänsehäufel

KAISER-
MÜHLEN

Donau

STADLAU

**Prater and
Riesenrad**

LEOPOLDSTADT

ASPERN

KunstHausWien

Hundertwasser-Haus

Wittgenstein Haus

LANDSTRASSE

**Wiener
Strassenbahnmuseum**

Donauinsel

Neue Donau

Lobau

Donau

ALBERN

SIMMERING

ROTH-
NEUSIEDL

esing

OBERLAA

Danube Cruise

View of the Danube Canal (left); Schwedenbrücke over the canal (right)

THE BASICS

➕ Off map to east
Vienna Cruises
www.ddsg-blue-danube.at
🕐 Several departures daily from Schwedenbrücke. Winter break
💶 Expensive
Twin City Liner
www.twincityliner.com
🕐 Several departures daily from Schwedenbrücke. Winter break
♿ Good; advance reservation essential
💶 Expensive
❓ Advance reservations recommended. Check frontier formalities for Slovak Republic before your trip
NationalparkBoot
☎ 4000-49480 (booking required)
🕐 2 May–26 Oct daily at 9 near Salztorbrücke. Cruise is 4 hours with 1 hour walk
💶 Expensive

HIGHLIGHTS

● UNO-City
● Kahlenberg and other hills
● Otto Wagner's Secessionist Nussdorf Lock and Lock House

Traditional Danube cruises start at Schwedenplatz. The route begins in the Donaukanal, then turns up the main river with a stop at the Reichsbrücke. It continues to Nussdorf and returns down the Donaukanal.

River cruises There are also special cruises, mainly in the evenings, offering Viennese music and more. Also leaving from Schwedenplatz is the NationalparkBoot, which takes you to the Danube National Park and its water meadows. The Park begins inside the city's boundaries and extends as far as the Slovak border.

Twin City Liner While the cruises within Vienna are not terribly exciting, the Twin City Liner offers an experience worth having. In little more than an hour, this huge catamaran rushes you to Bratislava, the capital of the Slovak Republic. It is very expensive (the train journey costs half the price) but you start and arrive right in the heart of both cities.

Donauinsel The artificial island between the Old and the New Danube has become popular for biking, picnicking and (at its southern tip) for nudism. One weekend in June each year, the island hosts what is said to be Europe's biggest outdoor festival of pop music (free access). There are modestly priced restaurants with international cuisine around the 'Copa Cagrana' between U1 stations Donauinsel and Kaisermühlen VIC.

Hundertwasser-Haus and KunstHausWien

Hundertwasser's career as an amateur architect began with his now-famous Hundertwasser-Haus in Vienna's Third District. It was built with the help of a professional architect, Josef Krawina, and opened in 1985.

The artist Born Friedrich Stowasser in 1928, the artist survived Nazi persecution in his native city of Vienna, the rest of his partly Jewish family perished in the Holocaust. In 1949, he took the name 'Friedensreich Hundertwasser' and in 1953 painted the first of his colourful spirals, with which he achieved overnight success. Over the years he became more and more involved in ecological initiatives as part of his artistic credo. He died on board the Queen Elizabeth II following a trip to New Zealand in 2000 and was buried there in his Garden of the Happy Dead—without a coffin, but with a tulip tree planted above his remains.

Hundertwasser-Haus The building reflects his opposition to pure functionalism and his view that 'the straight line is godless'. The house is not accessible (it is a block of council flats owned by the municipality). Instead the 'architect's' 'Kalke Village' across the street offers visitors the full Hundertwasser experience in all its whimsicality.

KunstHaus The KunstHaus is in a former furniture factory five minutes away from the Hundertwasserhaus. It was refurbished by the artist and now offers a survey of his life and work. Exhibitions pay homage to his unconventionality.

THE BASICS

Hundertwasser-Haus
www.hundertwasserhaus.info
➕ J4
✉ Kegelgasse 34/Löwengasse 41
👁 View from outside only
🚋 Tram N to Hetzgasse
♿ Good

KunstHausWien
www.kunsthauswien.com
➕ J4
✉ Untere Weissgerberstrasse
☎ 712 04 95
🕐 Daily 10–7
🍴 Café-restaurant
🚋 Trams N, O to Radetzkyplatz
♿ Good
💶 Expensive

TIP

● You can cruise the Danube from Schwedenplatz in MS *Vindobona*, renovated by Hundertwasser in 1995.

Kahlenberg

Karl-Marx-Hof (left); a Heuriger or wine tavern (right)

THE BASICS

🔹 Off map to northwest
🔹 U4 to Heiligenstadt then bus 38A

Beethoven Houses
Testament Museum:
✉ Probusgasse 6
🕐 Tue–Sun 10–1, 2–6
Heurigen Restaurant Mayer:
✉ Pfarrplatz 1
🕐 Daily from 4

Secessionist Villa Colony
✉ Steinfeldgasse 2, 4, 6, 7; Wollergasse 10
🚋 Tram 37 to Hohe Warte

HIGHLIGHTS

● View from Kahlenberg
● Hohe Warte Secessionist Villa Colony
● Karl-Marx-Hof tenement block

TIP

● The Heurigen Express is an open hop-on/hop-off shuttle bus connecting Nussdorf (Tram D last stop) and Kahlenberg (Apr–Oct daily 12–6 every full hour, moderate).

If you've had enough of culture and need some fresh air, visit the hills north of the city. You can drink a glass of wine in one of the villages and still see some fine architecture on the way.

Kahlenberg Imperial troops and their allies gathered here before liberating Vienna from the Turkish siege in 1683. The hill has become the most popular place from which to view the panorama of Vienna. In the diminutive Sobieski Chapel a fresco recalls the Polish contribution to the liberation of Vienna.

Heiligenstadt Probably the oldest of Vienna's wine growers' villages, Heiligenstadt is famous for the Heiligenstadt Testament that Beethoven wrote in his lodgings here. If this depresses you (and it is not a cheerful document) restore your spirits with a glass of wine in the charming Beethoven House *Heuriger* on Pfarrplatz.

Hohe Warte Secessionist Villa Colony Josef Hoffmann was a leading light of the Vienna Secession and co-founder of the Wiener Werkstätte. Four of his exquisite villas are located above Heiligenstadt's St. Michael's Church.

Karl-Marx-Hof Opposite the Heiligenstadt U-Bahn station is the most impressive dwelling-house of the 'Red Vienna' period in the 1920s. Many of these 'workers' fortresses' played a significant role in the 1934 Civil War between authoritarian Conservative and Social Democratic forces.

Prater and Riesenrad

The former imperial hunting grounds were opened to the public in 1766, and now include a chestnut avenue, a fairground and other leisure facilities. The world-famous amusement park has many diversions; the Ferris Wheel (the *Riesenrad*) is among the most popular.

The big wheel The Giant Ferris Wheel on the Prater, built in 1896 by Englishman Walter Basset, was where Harry Lime met his old friend in the film *The Third Man*. The wheel rotates at 75cm (29in) per second and offers great views across the city. Compartments can be hired for private celebrations and you can even get married in one!

Amusement park There has been ongoing debate between the entrepreneurs of the different attractions and the City of Vienna regarding the future of the 'Wurstelprater' fun-fair. Some wish to retain its traditional character, others want to modernize it. In fact traditional and new elements can be found here. Attractions include the *Geisterbahn* (ghost train), the old-fashioned *Ringelspiel* (merry-go-round) and the narrow-gauge *Liliputbahn* (381mm/15in), which starts from just behind the Giant Ferris Wheel. There are new dodgems and various 'test your strength' booths. Adherents of old and new meet on the neutral ground of the *Schweizerhaus* (Swiss House) to sample its notoriously gigantic *Stelze* (knuckle of pork) served with Czech beer.

THE BASICS

www.prater.at

🔛 K2

✉ East of Praterstern

🕐 Fun-fair: 15 Mar–end Oct daily. Giant Ferris Wheel: May–end Sep daily 9am–11.45pm; Mar–end Apr, Oct 10–9.45; Nov–end Feb 10–7.45. Closed 24, 31 Dec. Liliputbahn: daily 10–7

🚇 U1, U2, Schnellbahn to Praterstern

🚊 Trams O, 5, 21 to Praterstern

♿ Good

🎟 Ferris Wheel: moderate; Liliputbahn: inexpensive. Combined tickets available

HIGHLIGHTS

● Ferris Wheel
● *Liliputbahn*

TIP

● Take the *Liliputbahn* to Stadion, stroll down the Hauptallee and enjoy food at the Lusthaus (closed Wed).

Schloss Schönbrunn

HIGHLIGHTS

● Carriage museum (right of main entrance)
● Oriental panels, Vieux-Lacque Room
● Mirrors and frescoed ceiling in Great Gallery
● Park with statues and Gloriette

TIP

● The Roman Ruin (turn left from the Neptune Fountain) is in reality an artistic fake symbolizing the victory of Rome over Carthage. Close to it is the 'beautiful spring' itself (the *schöner Brunn*).

Schönbrunn is a cold, if imposing, palace, which was designed to show how many rooms a great monarch could afford. Yet Maria Theresa (1740–80) made it a cheerful home for her 12 surviving children.

Pacassi's palace The original designs for an imperial residence in the hunting park with the beautiful spring (the *schöner Brunn*, which gave the palace its name) were made by Johann Bernhard Fischer von Erlach in 1695, and were intended to rival Versailles. Only part of it was built when, between 1744 and 1749, Maria Theresa's court architect, Nikolaus Pacassi, revamped the design. His symmetrical, immense-ly long palace is a vast corridor of gilded and crimson displays—Japanese, Italian, Persian and

Relaxing with a book at Schönbrunn Palace; a statue in the garden; the imposing façade of Schloss Schönbrunn; view of the palace from the formal gardens; Carriage Museum; detail of the clock on the roof of the palace (clockwise from far left)

Indian works of art, ceiling frescos celebrating the Habsburgs and 18th-century furniture and porcelain. The palace looks out on a park with immaculate parterres and hedges and a vista of ornamental pools and fountains.

The park The 18th-century gardens were later partially restyled by Adrian van Steckhoven. On top of the hill stands the Gloriette, a piece of pure architecture, originally with no interior (only recently a café has been installed). It is worth climbing up to it for the view over the city. The zoo has also retained its 18th-century plan with a baroque pavilion in the middle, but now includes modern enclosures and buildings. A spectacular glass house was added in the 19th century and a labyrinth for kids has been added to the restored historical maze.

THE BASICS

www.schoenbrunn.at
✚ Off map to west
☎ 811 13-239
🕐 Palace: Apr–end Jun, Sep, Oct daily 8.30–5; Jul, Aug 8.30–6; Nov–end Mar 8.30–4.30. Carriage museum: Apr–end Oct 9–6, Nov–end Mar 10–4. Zoo: Apr–end Sep 9–6.30 or dusk. Park: 6.30–dusk
🍴 8 cafés and restaurants on premises
🚇 U4 to Schönbrunn or Hietzing (for palm house and zoo)
🚌 Bus 10A; trams 10, 58 to Schönbrunn
♿ Good
💶 Palace, zoo: expensive; park: free
❓ Audio guides. Tours can be booked online

More to See

AUGARTEN

www.augarten.at

Joseph II opened these gardens to the public in 1775. The porcelain factory in the Augarten Palace can be visited. The Augarten is also home to the Vienna Boys' Choir and an annexe of the Belvedere collection, Augarten Contemporary.

🚹 G1 🌳 Park 6–dusk

Porcelain Museum ✉ Obere Augartenstrasse 1A ☎ 211 24-200 🕐 Mon–Fri 9.30–5 🚇 U2 to Taborstrasse (from Jun 2008) 🚊 Tram N to Taborstrasse/ Obere Augartenstrasse 💷 Inexpensive

GÄNSEHÄUFEL

www.gänsehäufel.at

This is the Lido of Vienna, an island in the now dead arm of the river called the Alte Donau (Old Danube). It offers various facilities including an open-air pool with artificial waves and a water-chute, tennis, minigolf and even a place where rock climbers can try their skills. Extremely crowded on hot summer days.

🚹 Off map to northeast ✉ Moissigasse 21

☎ 269 90 16. Rock climbing requires prior appointment 0699/81813039 🚇 U1 to Kaisermühlen VIC (Vienna International Centre), then bus 92A to Schüttauplatz or occasional shuttle services 🦽 Good 💷 Moderate

KIRCHE AM STEINHOF

The weird and wonderful Steinhof Church was built for patients with mental illnesses in 1907. The interior is clinically white with special fittings, full of wonders from Secession artists—most notably Kolo Moser's glass-mosaic windows.

🚹 Off map to west ✉ Sozialmedizinisches Zentrum, Baumgartner Höhe 1 ☎ 910 60–11204 (Mon–Thu 8–3) 🕐 Sat 4pm–5pm (open access). Guided tour in German Sat 3pm or by prior arrangement 🚌 Buses 47A, 48A to Psychiatrisches Zentrum 🦽 None 💷 Tours inexpensive for groups of 10 people or more; expensive for smaller groups and tours in English

TECHNISCHES MUSEUM

www.technischesmuseum.at

Here you can explore the inventions

Augarten

and technical development of Austria past and present. The museum displays its items in user-friendly and spacious settings.

➕ Off map to west ✉ Mariahilferstrasse 212 ☎ 89998-6000 🕐 Mon–Fri 9–6, Sat–Sun, hols 10–6. Closed 1 Jan, 1 May, 1 Nov, 25, 31 Dec 🍴 Café 🚋 Trams 52, 58 from U3 Westbahnhof to Penzinger Strasse ♿ Good 💷 Expensive

WIENER STRASSENBAHNMUSEUM

www.wiener-tramwaymuseum.org

You can join a round-trip on a vintage tram starting from Karlsplatz and visit the Tramway Museum. Noteworthy in the museum are the horse- and steam-driven trams of the 19th century and a New York streetcar.

➕ L7 ✉ Ludwig-Kössler-Platz ☎ 7909-41800 🕐 May–early Oct Sat–Sun, hols 9–4 🚇 U3 to Schlachthausgasse 🚌 Bus 77A to Ludwig-Kössler-Platz 💷 Inexpensive

Oldtimer Tours 🕐 May–early Oct Sat 11.30, 1.30; Sun, hols also 9.30am. Start at Karlsplatz Otto Wagner Pavilions 🚇 U1, U2, U4 to Karlsplatz 💷 Moderate

WITTGENSTEIN HAUS

www.haus-wittgenstein.at

Ludwig Wittgenstein, one of the most famous philosophers of the 20th century, designed this austere house for his sister in the 1920s. The house reflects its creator's intellect; built in the Bauhaus style, it is curious rather than architecturally appealing.

➕ J5 ✉ Parkgasse 18 ☎ 713 3164 🕐 Mon–Fri 10–12, 3–4.30 🚇 U3 to Rochusgasse 💷 Free ❓ Accessible for functions of the Bulgarian Cultural Institute

WOTRUBA KIRCHE

This extraordinary modern church, designed by the sculptor Fritz Wotruba, seems to have been built with randomly jumbled concrete blocks and lit by arbitrarily placed narrow glass panels.

➕ Off map to southwest ✉ Georgsgasse/ Rysergasse (Mauer, 23rd District) ☎ 888 090 456. Guided tours 888 50 03 🕐 Sat, before church hols 2pm–8pm, Sun 9–5 🚌 Bus 60A to Kaserngasse from Schnellbahn Liesing or Atzgersdorf, then walk; tram 60 from Hietzing-Mauerer Lange Gasse, then walk

Wotruba Kirche

Excursions

THE BASICS

www.baden.at
Distance: 25km (16 miles)
Journey Time: 1 hour
☎ 02252/22 600-600
🚋 Badner Bahn (blue-white tram) from Oper. Supplementary fare from Vienna's city border
❓ Operetta performances in the Stadttheater end-Jun to mid-Sep

BADEN

A geological fault where the eastern edge of the Alps meets the Vienna Basin is responsible for the mineral springs at Baden, first exploited by the Romans. The now-sleepy town became a fashionable spa during the Biedermeier period (1815–48).

Mozart wrote his sublime *Ave Verum* chorus for the choir of the parish church. The town is full of Joseph Kornhäusel's neoclassical architecture. A tram (*Lokalbahn*) runs from Oper to Baden (25km/16 miles).

THE BASICS

Distance: 70km (43 miles)
Journey Time: 1 hour
🚆 From Wiener Südbahnhof to Bratislava Hlavná stanica (Main Station) or Petrzalka twice every hour
🚢 Twin City Liner (▷ 94)

BRATISLAVA

For a 1,000 years part of Hungary and for several centuries its capital, Bratislava became the capital of the newly independent Slovak Republic in 1993.

While the old city core has preserved its medieval and baroque charm, the outskirts of Bratislava have boomed since the fall of the Iron Curtain in 1989. A highlight is St. Martin's Cathedral, where 11 kings of Hungary were crowned. The views over the city from either the castle terraces or the tower of the Novy most (New Bridge) are spectacular.

THE BASICS

Distance: 35km (22 miles)
Journey Time: 1 hour
☎ 02258-8703
🚆 From Südbahnhof, Südtirolerplatz (U1) or Wien Meidling (U6) to Mödling, then bus 365
🕐 Mon–Sat at 10, 11, 2, 3, 4. Sun, hols no tour at 10
💶 Moderate

HEILIGENKREUZ

This abbey, whose name 'Holy Cross' is derived from the fragment of the True Cross preserved in a tabernacle on the main altar, was founded in 1133 by the Cistercians.

The church has a lovely Romanesque nave and Gothic choir. Later baroque features include a Trinity Column in the courtyard.

KLOSTERNEUBURG

Legend has it that this monastery was founded on the spot where Margrave Leopold III discovered the veil of his wife Agnes after the wind had blown it away when they were out hunting.

The small winegrowers' town upstream from the capital was the residence of the Babenbergs before they moved to Vienna. In the 18th century, Charles VI planned to turn it into an Austrian Escorial. The Verdun altar with its gilded copper plates from 1181 and the 'Archduke's hat', the modest crown of the Duchy of Austria, are the most interesting exhibits. A new attraction in the town is the private Essl Collection of contemporary art (An der Donau-Au 1; 02243-370 50-150; Tue–Sun 10–6, Wed until 9; moderate, Wed 6–9pm free).

THE BASICS

www.stift-klosterneuburg.at
Distance: 10km (6 miles)
Journey Time: 20 min by train or bus
☎ 02243-411-0
🚌 Bus 239 from Heiligenstadt to Niedermark
🚊 From Spittelau (U4, U6) to Klosterneuburg-Kierling
Monastery
🕐 Daily 9–6. Closed 25, 26 Dec; 24, 31 Dec from 12; 1 Jan from 1
💰 Expensive; Dec–Apr moderate

LAXENBURG

The former imperial summer resort at Laxenburg has three palaces to visit and an extensive English park.

You come first to the baroque Blue Court (which is not blue at all). Inside the park, to the right, you will find the Old Castle, and to your left the 19th-century neo-Gothic folly known as the Franzensburg. The latter boasts a fake medieval dungeon, complete with a knight in chains and realistic groans in the background. It is located on an island reached by a cable ferry, or via a bridge from the rear of the park. You can also take a rowboat and discover the hidden beauties of the lake, including a vast romantic grotto.

The Old Palace now houses the Austrian Film Archive, while the Blue Court is the seat of the IIASA, the International Institute for Applied Systems Analysis. In the surroundings of an imperial pleasure ground, experts ponder the problems of today's environmental, economic and social changes.

THE BASICS

www.laxenburg.at
www.schlosslaxenburg.at
Distance: 25km (16 miles)
Journey Time: 30 min
🚌 Bus 566 from U1 Südtirolerplatz, hourly
☎ 02236-71226
🕐 Park: daily dawn–dusk. Franzensburg: Easter–Oct daily 11, 2, 3
💰 Park, ferry, Franzensburg tour: inexpensive. Panorama train: moderate

THE BASICS

www.ddsg-blue-danube.at
www.bradner.at
Distance: 85km (53 miles)
Journey Time: 1.5 hours
by train to Melk or Krems
🚇 From Westbahnhof (U3, U6) or Spittelau (U4, U6) or Franz-Josefs-Bahnhof (Trams D, 5)
🕓 Cruises: mid-Apr to 26 Oct. Reserve in advance

MELK AND WACHAU VALLEY

The huge baroque monastery at Melk commands the entrance to the Wachau Valley on the Danube.

You can take a cruise either from Melk downstream to Krems in the Wachau or from Krems upstream to Melk. Stroll through the narrow streets of Krems or see an art exhibition in the Kunsthalle. The landscape of the river valley is adorned with vineyards, picturesque villages and castle ruins such as Dürnstein, where King Richard the Lionheart was held prisoner in 1192–93.

THE BASICS

Distance: 20km (13 miles)
Journey Time: 1 hour
☎ 02236-26364
🕓 Apr–Oct daily 9–5; Nov–Mar Mon–Fri 9–12, 1–3, Sat–Sun, hols 9–3.30
🚇 Schnellbahn to Mödling then bus 364 or 365

SEEGROTTE HINTERBRÜHL

Situated in a former gypsum mine, this is Europe's biggest underground lake.

Water accumulated in it after a blasting operation in 1912, and has to be pumped out daily (there are seven sources but no outflow). In World War II, aircraft were produced in the grotto by 2,000 workers, but nowadays tourists cruise the waters in small boats.

THE BASICS

www.semmering.at
www.semmeringbahn.at
Distance: 100km (66 miles)
Journey Time: 2 hours
🚇 From Südbahnhof or Meidling approx. every hour; few are direct

SEMMERING

Completed in 1854, the Semmering railway, which runs southwest from Vienna to the Italian border, was the first mountain railway on the continent.

It is still admired for its sophisticated engineering in a mountainous landscape. Semmering station exudes the atmosphere of excursion hotels and villas from the turn of the 20th century, the resort having once been a preferred summer retreat for the well-to-do from Vienna and Budapest.

In 1998 the historic Semmering Railway was added to the UNESCO World Heritage list. Every second year or so, the World Cup downhill ski races take place on the Hirschenkogel at the top of the Semmering pass.

Shopping

MANNER FABRIKSVERKAUF
Locally produced Neopolitan wafers sold in attractive gift packs, plus Ildefonso chocolates.
🔲 Off map at A3
✉ Wilheminestrasse 6
☎ 488 22 ◐ Mon–Thu 9–5, Fri 9–2 🚋 Tram 44 to Wilhelminenstrasse/Wattgasse

NATURPRODUKTE WALLNER
If you like a sense of well-being, you will appreciate the whole and organic foods, alternative beauty therapies and baby food sold here.
🔲 E8 ✉ Wiedner

Hauptstrasse 66 ☎ 586 06 71 ◐ Mon–Fri 9–6, Sat 9–5 🚋 Trams 62, 65 to Johann-Strauss-Gasse

ROCK-SHOP
A paradise for vinyl

COSTLY LEATHER

Fashion items such as leather goods are expensive in Vienna. The best selections and prices are found at chain stores like Humanic, in the vast shopping mall on the southern outskirts of the city (✉ Shopping City Süd, Vösendorf 🚌 Ikea bus from the Oper).

---

collectors. Oldies from the 1950s to the 1970s, mostly singles hits.
🔲 H1 ✉ Taborstrasse 70
☎ 216 89 93 ◐ Mon–Fri 9–12, 2–6, Sat 9–12 🚋 Tram N to Heinestrasse

WIENER PORZELLANFABRIK
You can also buy Augarten porcelain direct from the factory. Seconds sell at a 20 per cent discount.
🔲 G1 ✉ Wiener Porzellanmanufaktur, Obere Augartenstrasse 1 ☎ 211 24-200 ◐ Mon–Fri 10–5 🚋 Tram N to Obere Augartenstrasse

Entertainment and Nightlife

ARENA
A music and arts building.
🔲 M8/9 ✉ Baumgasse 80
☎ 798 85 95 ◐ May–Sep daily from 2pm (4pm in winter) Ⓤ U3 to Erdberg

CITY & COUNTRY GOLF CLUB AM WIENERBERG
In the southern suburbs of Vienna.
🔲 Off map at E9 ✉ Gutheil Schoder-Gasse 9 ☎ 661 23 🚌 Bus 16A to Gutheil Schoder-Gasse

FRITZ EPPEL
Boats for rental.
🔲 Off map at L1

✉ Wagramer Strasse 48A
☎ 263 3530 Ⓤ U1 to Alte Donau

SCHÖNBRUNNER SCHLOSSTHEATER
In the rococo theatre, the Wiener Kammeroper performs lighter opera and operettas throughout July and August.
🔲 Off map at A9 ✉ Schloss Schönbrunn ☎ 711 55-158 Ⓤ U4 to Schönbrunn

U4
An enduring and continually fashionable dance club with live music most nights. Next door is a bar.

🔲 Off map at A9
✉ Schönbrunner Strasse 222
☎ 815 8307 ◐ Daily 10pm–5am Ⓤ U4 to Meidlinger Hauptstrasse

WIENER STADTHALLE (HALLE C)
Major municipal sports complex with an ice rink and Olympic-size swimming pool.
🔲 A5/6 ✉ Vogelweidplatz 14 ☎ 981 000 ◐ Mon–Fri 1.30–5, Sat–Sun, hols 8–12, 1–5 Ⓤ U6 🚋 Tram 49 to Burggasse/Stadthalle/Urban-Loritz-Platz

Restaurants

ALTER BACH-HENGL (€€)

www.bach-hengl.at
This is a typical, family-run *Heuriger*, with garden tables in summer. Also traditional *Schrammel* music, hot-and-cold buffet and *Gemischter Satz* (the local white-wine cuvée) to drink.

🔛 Off map at F1
✉ Sandgasse 7–9 ☎ 320 24 39 🕐 4pm–midnight
🚋 Tram 38 from Schottentor to end stop Grinzing

DOMMAYER (€€)

Close to Schönbrunn and the zoo, and revived under the new owners (Oberlaa Konditorei). Once a month, the female ensemble Wiener Walzmädchen gives a performance at Vienna's oldest music café. Johann Strauss once played here.

🔛 Off map at A9
✉ Auhofstrasse 2 (Hietzing) ☎ 877 54 65-0 🕐 Daily 7am–10pm 🚇 U4 to Hietzing 🚋 Tram 58 to Dommayergasse

DONAUTURM (€€€)

www.donauturm.at
Dine in the revolving restaurant at the top of the Danube Tower. If you're so inclined, there's bungee jumping from a platform. Also the 'Stair Run' in November.

🔛 Off map at L1
✉ Donauturmstrasse 4
🕐 Daily 11.30–3, 6–midnight; observation deck: 10am–midnight 🚌 Bus 20B from U1 Kaisermühlen VIC to Donauturm (watch for direction)

FUHRGASSL-HUBER (€€)

www.fuhrgassl-huber.at
One of the most congenial taverns in Neustift's long main street. The same family also runs an excellent pension close by.

🔛 Off map at D1
✉ Neustift am Walde 68
☎ 440 14 05 🕐 Mon–Sat 2pm–midnight, Sun, hols 12–12 🚇 U4, U6 to Spittelau then bus 35A to Neustift am Walde

HEURIGEN

A *Heuriger* is a tavern in its own vineyard, traditionally selling only the current year's *Heuer* (wine). When open, a *Heuriger* is *ausg'steckt*, indicated by a bunch of fir twigs hung outside the door. The basic wine is *Gemischter Satz*, a white blend of local grapes. Roast meats, cheeses and salads are served in most *Heurigen*. The warm atmosphere is quintessentially Viennese with *Schrammelmusik* playing.

MAYER AM PFARRPLATZ (€€)

www.pfarrplatz.at
The most famous *Heuriger* in Heiligenstadt. Beethoven worked on his Ninth Symphony in the house.

🔛 Off map at D1
✉ Heiligenstädter Pfarrplatz 2
☎ 370 33 61 or 370 12 87
🕐 Daily 4pm–midnight. Closed Christmas to mid-Jan
🚇 U4 to Heiligenstadt then bus 38A to Fernsprechamt Heiligenstadt

PLACHUTTA (€€€)

www.plachutta.at
If you want to sample the famous *Wiener Tafelspitz* (boiled beef) at its most luxurious, as well as other beef specialties, this is the place. The restaurant is in the elegant suburb of Hietzing close to Schönbrunn.

🔛 Off map at A9
✉ Auhofstrasse 1 ☎ 877 70 87 🕐 Daily 11.30–3, 6–midnight 🚇 U4 to Hietzing 🚋 Tram 58 to Dommayergasse

ZIMMERMANN (€€)

A quiet *Heuriger* off the beaten track and close to the Beethoven House, where the composer's tragic Heiligenstadt Testament letter was written.

🔛 Off map at D1
✉ Armbrustergasse 5 ☎ 370 22 11 🕐 Mon–Sat 5pm–2am
🚇 U4 to Heiligenstadt then bus 38A from to Armbrustergasse

In Vienna there is an extremely broad choice of hotels, and most of them succeed in combining old-fashioned charm with modern comforts.

Introduction

In Vienna tourist accommodation ranges from luxury hotels in baroque palaces to much smaller and friendly establishments with a local character, some family run.

Tradition

At the crossroads of Central Europe, Vienna has a long tradition of welcoming guests, from medieval crusaders and merchants to the high-ranking diplomats, officials of international bodies and tourists of today. The names of some hotels such as König von Ungarn (King of Hungary), Das Triest, Ambassador or Imperial reflect the city's ancient geographical and historical significance. To stay in one of these is to be transported back in time. These traditional hotels have nevertheless been tastefully modernized, so that they fully meet the demands of today's jet set.

Millionaires and Expense Accounts

Vienna has become one of the world's top venues for international conferences and is one of the three bases of the UN. It attracts well-to-do and influential visitors from Arab nations, due to OPEC headquarters located here. The new millionaires from the post-Communist countries of Eastern Europe, plus many of their compatriots, have also become regular visitors. To cater to this new clientele, recent hotel development has been in the mid-range and luxury categories. Nevertheless there are plenty of budget hotels and hostels.

Viennese hotels: Kaiserin Elisabeth; Doint Biedermeier; Imperial; Sacher (top to bottom)

HOTEL LOCATIONS

Most of the famous hotels are inside or on the Ringstrasse. This includes traditional 19th-century luxury hotels like Sacher, Imperial or Bristol, but also newcomers like the Marriot and Le Meridien. Hotels outside the Ringstrasse are less formal and often located on attractive smaller streets or courtyards. Hotels in the outskirts of the city may offer a more parklike environment or gardens, as well as lower prices. Student hostels are mostly situated in the lively 'Inner Districts' between the Ringstrasse and the Gürtel (Ring Road).

Budget Hotels

PRICES

Expect to pay under €110 for a double room per night in a budget hotel.

ACADEMIA

www.academia-hotels.co.at
Basically a students' home, this huge hotel is open in July, August and September only. Situated in a quiet residential area, it has a terrace on the 11th floor. Good tram and bus connections to the city hub, Belvedere and Südbahnhof.

☎ C4 ✉ Pfeilgasse 3a (between Lerchengasse and Strozzigasse) ☎ 401 76; fax 401 76-20 ▣ Bus 13A to Ledererergasse/Josefstädter Strasse or Theater in der Josefstadt; tram J to Ledererergasse/Josefstädter Strasse

KUGEL

www.hotelkugel.at
Extremely good value near the lively Spittelberg area, which is full of open-air restaurants in summer. 38 rooms.

☎ C5/6 ✉ Siebensterngasse 43/corner Neubaugasse ☎ 523 33 55; fax 523 33 55-5 ◉ Closed early Jan–early Feb ▣ Bus 13A, tram 49 to Neubaugasse/Westbahnhofstrasse

LEHRERHAUS

www.lhv.at
Run by the Association for Teachers' Accommodation, everybody is welcome in this pension in the middle-class suburb of the Josefstadt just behind the Parliament and Rathaus. Simple accommodation best suited for low budget tourists interested in culture. Vienna's English Theatre is based here.

☎ D4 ✉ Lange Gasse 20–22/ Josefsgasse ☎ 403 23 58-100 or 403 23 58-0; fax 403 23 58-700 ▣ U2 ▣ Tram J to Rathaus

MATAUSCHEK

www.hotel-matauschek.at
Small family-run hotel reached with U3 (direction Otakring) or tram 10 from Hietzing (Schönbrunn zoo). Caters specifically for families with children. The owner cooks the meals himself.

☎ Off map at A6 ✉ Breitenseer Strasse 14

IN SEARCH OF GOOD VALUE

Other than youth hostels, there is little inexpensive accommodation in Vienna. At the same time, there are still hotels with less than friendly service that nevertheless charge the (high) going rate. The Viennese themselves remark darkly that the world of hotels is under the eternal sway of the mythical 'King Nepp' (from *neppen*, meaning to overcharge). Few escape his tyrannous rule, but there are several (some are listed here) that do try hard to offer value for money and friendly service.

☎ 982 35 32 ▣ U3 to Hütteldorfer Strasse ▣ Trams 10, 49 to Hütteldorfer Strasse

PENSION AM OPERNECK

In this seven-room bed and breakfast, they bring breakfast to your room.

☎ F5 ✉ Kärntner Strasse 47 ☎ 512 93 10; fax 512 93 10-20 ▣ U1, U2, U4 to Oper

PRIVATE ROOMS

www.netland.at/wien/apartment-vienna.htm
The website of the official Apartment & Vacation Rental Owner Organization of Vienna helps you book one of the 250 Vienna apartments, vacation rentals and bed and breakfasts in all districts of the city.

WOMBAT'S HOSTELS

www.wombats.at
Two locations close to Westbahnhof and with direct transport to most of the major sights. Simple, but clean and friendly. Rooms have one to six beds, all with their own toilet and shower. The WomBar in the new Lounge is for beer-drinkers who would like to swap experiences and local knowledge with other young people.

☎ A7 ✉ The Lounge: Mariahilferstrasse 137; The Base: Grangasse 6 ☎ 897 23 36; fax 897 25 77 ▣ U3, U6 to Westbahnhof ▣ Trams 5, 6, 18, 52, 58 to Westbahnhof

Mid-Range Hotels

PRICES

Expect to pay between €110 and €218 per night for a double room in a mid-range hotel.

ALTSTADT VIENNA
www.altstadt.at
Small but refined (37 rooms), the beautifully furnished upper floors of this 18th-century house are an informal, friendly breakfast-only hotel.
➕ D4 ✉ Kirchengasse 41
☎ 526 66 66; fax 523 49 01
🚌 Bus 48A to Kellermanngasse

ALTWIENERHOF
www.altwienerhof.at
This one is for food lovers; bargain rates, in view of the fine restaurant. The 26 rooms have an opulent *belle époque* look.
➕ A8 ✉ Herklotzgasse 6
☎ 892 60 00; fax 892 60 00-8
🚇 U3, U6 🚌 Bus 57A, trams 6, 18 to Gumpendorfer Strasse

AMADEUS
www.hotel-amadeus.at
A small, but distinguished bed and breakfast just a few steps from the heart of the city, the Amadeus attracts especially artists, intellectuals and businesspeople. A friendly welcome is guaranteed and the pleasant surroundings will add to a comfortable stay.
➕ F4 ✉ Wildpretmarkt 5
☎ 533 8738; fax 533 8738-38
🚇 U1, U3 to Stephansplatz

ERZHERZOG RAINER
http://schick-hotels.at
This is a comfortable Best Western but is slightly old-fashioned. It is close to the Austrian Chamber of Commerce and the Technical University.
➕ F7 ✉ Wiedner Hauptstrasse 27-29 ☎ 22 111; fax 22 111-350 🚇 U1 to Taubstummengasse 🚋 Trams 62, 65, Badner Bahn to Paulanergasse

GARTENHOTEL GLANZING
www.gartenhotel-glanzing.at
A peaceful 1920s cube-like villa softened by climbing vines. Far from downtown. 14 rooms.
➕ Off map at D1
✉ Glanzinggasse 23 ☎ 470 42 72; fax 470 42 72-14
🚌 Bus 35A to Glanzing

HOTEL AM SCHUBERTRING
www.schubertring.at
Adolf Loos-style bar and

DAY AND NIGHT
The Viennese tend to get up rather early, but this works to the tourist's advantage, as public transport will be much more comfortable when you are heading for your first sight. By the same token, many Viennese go relatively early to bed and lots of restaurants therefore start serving supper quite early. Nevertheless for night owls there are plenty of bars and a substantial network of night-long transport.

39 pleasant rooms. Much patronized by visiting musicians. No restaurant.
➕ G6 ✉ Schubertring 11
☎ 717 02-0; fax 713 99 66
🚋 Trams 1, 2 to Schwarzenbergplatz

HOTEL JÄGER
www.hoteljaeger.at
A welcoming Best Western 18-room hotel in a large villa with a lovely garden. Ideal for families but far from the middle of the city.
➕ Off map at A2
✉ Hernalser Hauptstrasse 187
☎ 486 66 20-0; fax 486 66 20-8 🚋 Tram 43 or Schnellbahn to Hernals

HOTEL-PENSION ARENBERG
www.arenberg.at
A Best Western hotel; unpretentious and friendly with 22 rooms.
➕ H4 ✉ Stubenring 2
☎ 512 52 91; fax 513 93 56
🚋 Trams 1, 2 to Stubenring

HOTEL-PENSION MUSEUM
www.tiscover.com/
hotelpension.museum
Art lovers and academics are attracted to this old-fashioned pension with 15 large rooms. Close to the Kunsthistorisches Museum (▷ 52–53).
➕ D5 ✉ Museumstrasse 3
☎ 523 44 26; fax 523 44 26-30 🚇 U2, U3 to Volkstheater

HOTEL RÖMISCHER KAISER
www.hotel-romischer-kaiser.at
A modest baroque palace

in the old city. Delightful—all crimson fabrics and chandeliers. No restaurant. 24 rooms.

✚ F5 ✉ Annagasse 16 ☎ 512 77 51-0; fax 512 77 51-13 🚇 U1, U3 to Stephansplatz

HOTEL WANDL
www.hotel-wandl.com
Popular hotel with 138 rooms next to Peterskirche in a partly 12th-century building.

✚ F4 ✉ Petersplatz 9 ☎ 534 55-0; fax 534 55-77 🚇 U1, U3 to Stephansplatz

KAISERIN ELISABETH
www.kaiserinelisabeth.at
This 63-room hotel has a whiff of imperial nostalgia; popular with regular Vienna visitors. A good choice if you want to be immersed in the Altstadt atmosphere.

✚ F4 ✉ Weinburggasse 3 ☎ 515 26-0; fax 515 26-7 🚇 U1, U3 to Stephansplatz

KÖNIG VON UNGARN
www.kvu.at
An 18th-century building next to the Figarohaus. Rooms ring an airy, glassed-in courtyard. Prestigious restaurant. 33 rooms.

✚ G4 ✉ Schulerstrasse 10 ☎ 515 84-0; fax 515 84-8 🚇 U1, U3 to Stephansplatz

PENSION LANDHAUS FUHRGASSL-HUBER
www.fuhrgassl-huber.at
Located in a wine village by the Vienna Woods. With its peasant-style

furniture and a summer courtyard, this one is special. 38 rooms.

✚ Off map at D1 ✉ Rathstrasse 24, Neustift am Walde ☎ 440 30 33; fax 440 27 14 🚌 Bus 35A to Agnesgasse

PENSION NOSSEK
Good location in the heart of the city; the pedestrianized area ensures quiet. The 26 rooms range from spacious to compact. Pleasant service. Reserve well in advance.

✚ F4 ✉ Graben 17 ☎ 533 70 41; fax 535 36 46 🚇 U1, U3 to Stephansplatz

PENSION PERTSCHY
www.pertschy.com
Pleasant and friendly, this pension is just off the Graben. The 50 rooms are spacious with period furniture.

✚ F4 ✉ Habsburgergasse 5 ☎ 534 49-0; fax 534 49-49 🚇 U1, U3 to Stephansplatz

SUBURBS
While luxury hotels are clearly concentrated in the Inner City or Ringstrassen area, many mid-range ones are to be found in the suburbs. Access to the city centre is not a problem, as most of them are near underground or tram stations. They also will seduce you to explore quite charming areas not otherwise visited.

WIMBERGER ARCOTEL
www.arcotel.at
This modern hotel with 225 rooms offers good traffic connections and convenient accommodation at reasonable prices. It is preferred by local and international sportspeople and artists performing at the nearby Stadthalle, Vienna's biggest event hall. From the upper floors there is a nice outlook to the Wienerwald (Vienna Woods).

✚ B6 ✉ Neubaugürtel 34-36 ☎ 521 65-0; fax 521 65-810 🚇 U6 to Neubaugasse/Stadthalle 🚊 Trams 6, 18, 49 to Urban-Loritz-Platz

ZIPSER
www.zipser.at
The Zipser is a premium address for cultural tourists who also want to enjoy the special flair of Vienna's smartest suburb, Josefstadt. The area has a pleasant villagey and funky atmosphere. There are numerous restaurants in Josefstadt, which also offers the Theater in der Josefstadt and the baroque Piarist Church on nearby Jodok-Fink-Platz.

✚ C3 ✉ Lange Gasse 49 ☎ 404 54-0; fax 404 54-13 🚇 U2 to Rathaus 🚊 Tram J to Rathaus

Luxury Hotels

PRICES

Expect to pay over €218 per night for a double room at a luxury hotel.

BRISTOL
www.starwoodhotels.com
Old-fashioned elegance on the Ringstrasse. Its restaurant, Korso bei der Oper (▷ 44), is one of the best in Vienna.
🛨 F5 ⊠ Kärntner Ring 1 ☎ 515 16-0; fax 515 16-550 🚇 U1, U2, U4 to Karlsplatz/Oper

HOTEL IMPERIAL
www.starwoodhotels.com
This former palace on the Ringstrasse is also the official State Hotel where visiting dignitaries stay. Hitler lodged here just after his annexation of Austria.
🛨 F6 ⊠ Kärntner Ring 16 ☎ 501 10-0; fax 501 10-410 🚇 U1, U2, U4 to Karlsplatz 🚋 Trams 1, 2, D to Schwarzenbergplatz

HOTEL SACHER
www.sacher.com
The 108 rooms are not generous, but Sacher is Vienna's most celebrated hotel—and not only because of the cake.
🛨 F5 ⊠ Philharmoniker-strasse 4 ☎ 514 56-0; fax 514 56-810 🚇 U1, U2, U4 to Karlsplatz/Oper

IM PALAIS SCHWARZENBERG
www.palais-schwarzenberg.com
In the Fischer von Erlachs'

palace (▷ 85), this is probably the most elegant address in the city. Hotel and restaurant to reopen in 2009.
🛨 G6 ⊠ Schwarzenberg-platz 9 ☎ 798 45 15-0; fax 798 47 14 🚋 Tram D to Gusshausstrasse

INTERCONTINENTAL WIEN
www.ichotelsgroup.com
You'll find a bit more than chain-hotel efficiency here. The Vier Jahres-zeiten restaurant is superb. 453 rooms.
🛨 G6 ⊠ Johannesgasse 28 ☎ 711 22-0; fax 713 44 89 🚇 U4 to Stadtpark

MARRIOTT VIENNA
www.marriott.com/vieat
Excellent business facilities and 313 rooms.
🛨 G5 ⊠ Parkring 12A ☎ 515 18-0; fax 515 18-6736 🚇 U3 to Stubentor 🚋 Trams 1, 2 to Weihburggasse

HOTEL SACHER

Sacher was once famous for its *chambres séparées*, where aristocrats 'entertained' dancers. It was founded in 1876 by the son of the cook to Prince Metternich and carried on by his formidable, cigar-smoking widow, Anna, who ruled her hotel and guests with an iron rod. Just after World War I, Anna single-handedly held off a mob of rioting workers, but she also had a strong social conscience and fed the poor from the kitchen.

MERCURE GRAND HOTEL BIEDERMEIER WIEN
www.accor.com
This period town house, with Biedermeier furniture is an oasis of tranquillity.
🛨 J5 ⊠ Landstrasser Hauptstrasse 28, Ungargasse 13 ☎ 716 71-0; fax 716 71-503 🚇 U3 to Rochusgasse, U4 to Landstrasse/Wien Mitte 🚌 Bus 74A to Weyrgasse

RADISSON SAS-PALAIS HOTEL
www.radissonsas.com
Distinguished hotel famous for solid service and its excellent restaurant, Le Siècle im Ersten.
🛨 G5 ⊠ Palais Henckel von Donnersmarck, Weihburggasse 32, Parkring 16 ☎ 515 17-0; fax 512 22 16 🚇 U3 to Stubentor

RENAISSANCE WIEN
www.marriott.com
This luxury hotel is slightly impersonal but a plus is the indoor pool. 309 rooms.
🛨 Off map at A9 ⊠ Linke Wienzeile/Ullmannstrasse 71 ☎ 891 02-0; fax 891 02-100 🚇 U4 to Meidlinger Hauptstrasse

DAS TRIEST
www.dastriest.at
Terence Conran meets Wiener Modern. This postmodern conversion of an old coaching inn has an excellent restaurant. 72 rooms.
🛨 F6 ⊠ Wiedner Haupt-strasse 12 ☎ 589 18-0; fax 589 18-18 🚋 Trams 62, 65, Badner Bahn to Resselgasse

WHERE TO STAY LUXURY HOTELS

This section supplies you with all the practical information needed to make your stay in Vienna as comfortable as possible, including tips for using public transport, when to go and money matters.

Planning Ahead

When to Go

Most of the important festivals and events are held in spring and summer. The main opera and concert seasons kick-off in autumn. Some prime attractions (such as the Lipizzaners and the Vienna Boys Choir) take a summer break and may be on tour some months.

> **TIME**
>
> Vienna is one hour ahead of the UK, six hours ahead of New York and nine hours ahead of Los Angeles.

AVERAGE DAILY MAXIMUM TEMPERATURES											
JAN	FEB	MAR	APR	MAY	JUN	JUL	AUG	SEP	OCT	NOV	DEC
34°F	37°F	48°F	59°F	66°F	73°F	79°F	77°F	68°F	59°F	45°F	39°F
1°C	3°C	9°C	15°C	19°C	23°C	26°C	25°C	20°C	215°C	7°C	4°C

Spring (March to May) is rainy and sometimes fairly cool until mid-April.

Summer (June to August), every year seems to get hotter!

Autumn (September to October) is the most pleasant time to visit when it is not too hot and mostly dry.

Winter (November to February) can be bitterly cold, often with heavy snow from late December.

If you suffer from migraines or circulation problems you may be affected by the *Föhn* wind blowing off the Alps.

WHAT'S ON

February *Opernball* (Opera Ball): The highlight of the social calendar.

March–April *Osterklang Wien*: Sacred music for Easter in St. Stephen's, the Musikverein and elsewhere.

March–June & September–December *Equestrian ballet*: Performances by the Lipizzaners.

April *Frühlingsfestival* (mid-Apr to mid-May): Concerts in the Musikverein and Konzerthaus.

May *Maifest* (1 May): Celebrations mostly in the Prater. The Socialist Democrats' march on the Ringstrasse looks increasingly anachronistic.

City Marathon: Reichsbrücke to the Rathaus.

Wiener Festwochen (May to mid-Jun): Arts festival.

June *Open-air festival* (end Jun): Pop music on the Danube Island.

July *Jazz Fest Wien*: At the Opera House and the Volkstheater.

Klangbogen Wien (Jul–Aug): Classical concerts and operas at the Theater an der Wien.

Music on Film (Jul–Aug): Films (mostly opera) on a screen in front of the Rathaus.

Summer Operetta (mid-Jun to mid-Aug): At the Schönbrunner Schlosstheater.

October *Viennale:* Film Festival.

November *Wien Modern*: One of Europe's biggest festivals of contemporary music.

November–December *Christkindlmarkt* (mid-Nov to 24 Dec): A Christmas fair in front of the Rathaus.

New Year's Eve *Silvesterpfad*: Shows and concerts.

Die Fledermaus: At the State Opera.

Vienna Online

www.austria-info.com
An easy-to-navigate site that gives information on all types of holidays in Austria, including car, motorcycle and hiking itineraries. Other features include a listing of events, weather forecasts, water temperatures in the lakes, plus webcam pictures of towns, landscapes and buildings.

www.vienna.at
Available in German only, this site offers diverse general information on the city from politics and culture to urban development and the environment. The restaurant and eaterie listings are rather brief.

www.info.wien.at
A site with images of Vienna and with information on sightseeing, eating out, culture, and more. Useful for locating theatre booking offices and (in some cases) booking online. The 72-hour itinerary is a good tour for first-time visitors and those with limited time.

www.vienneseball.org
Details on how to join a party (organized by the Johann Strauss society of Great Britain) for one of the celebrated Vienna winter balls. It includes history of the balls, instructions about etiquette for participants and much more.

www.hungrymonster.com
A fun site for those interested in international cuisine, including Viennese.

www.falter.at
Look under 'Wien, wie es isst' for details of recommended restaurants (German only).

www.tourist-net.co.at/coffee
This general tourist site for Austria has some good material about Vienna's coffeehouses and a useful listing of some of the better known and most atmospheric.

USEFUL WEBSITES

www.fodors.com
A complete travel-planning site. Research prices and weather; book air tickets, cars and rooms; pose questions to fellow visitors; and find links to other sites.

www.oeamtc.at
Invaluable for motorists, this site (only in German) informs about the current state of traffic on Austrian roads, roadworks, weather conditions and much more. The visuals will help non-German speakers.

CYBER CAFÉS

BIGNET.cafe
F4 ⬛ Hoher Markt 8–9
☎ 533 29 59 ⏰ Daily
10am–midnight

Coffeeshop Company
G3 ⬛ Rabensteig 8
☎ 532 83 61 ⏰ Mon–Thu
7am–9pm, Fri 7am–11pm, Sat 10am–11pm, Sun and hols 10–9

g-zone
D3 ⬛ Universitäts-strasse 11 ⏰ Mon–Fri
10am–11pm, Sat–Sun
2pm–11pm

Internetcafe Surfland
F5 ⬛ Krugerstrasse 10
☎ 512 77 01 ⏰ Mon–Fri
9am–11pm, Sat–Sun
10am–11pm

Getting There

ENTRY REQUIREMENTS

Visitors from the UK, EU countries, the US and Canada need a passport (valid for at least six months) but do not need a visa. For the latest passport and visa information, check your relevant embassy website (Britain: www.britishembassy.gov.uk; USA: www.usembassy.gov)

VACCINATIONS

Some wooded areas of Austria are home to *Zecken*, a kind of tick whose bite can transmit encephalitis, which in a few cases proves fatal. Enquire at the Austrian consulate about inoculation.

CUSTOMS REGULATIONS

Duty-free limits for non-European Union visitors are: 200 cigarettes or 250g of tobacco or 50 cigars; 2 litres of wine and 1 litre of spirits.

AIRPORT

Vienna International Airport is 19km (12 miles) east of the city at Schwechat. The airport has extensive shopping facilities, restaurants, bars, newsstands and car rental desks.

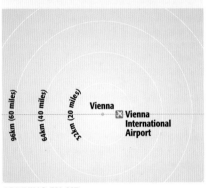

96km (60 miles)   64km (40 miles)   32km (20 miles)   Vienna   Vienna International Airport

ARRIVING BY AIR

For arrivals information at Vienna International Airport ☎ 7007 22233 (24 hours); www.viennaairport.com. The convenient option for transport to the city is the Vienna Airport Lines bus (☎ 93000/2300) to and from UNO-City, Schwedenplatz, Südbahnhof and Westbahnhof (20–30 minutes, €6). The CAT express train (www.cityairporttrain.at) to Wien Mitte costs €9 and runs between 5.30am and 11.30pm; the journey lasts 16 minutes. The S-Bahn (Schnellzug) rapid transit service is slower (24 minutes) but cheaper (€3) and runs from the Flughafen via Wien Mitte and Wien Nord to Floridsdorf. Timetables of the above services are shown on the website of Flughafen Wien. Taxis from the airport cost €35–€45.

ARRIVING BY TRAIN

International trains arrive at the Westbahnhof (Western Railway Station) and Südbahnhof (Southern Railway Station). Confusingly, trains do not necessarily only go south from the Südbahnhof or west from the Westbahnhof. Most trains of the Austrian Federal Railways (Österreichische Bundesbahnen, ÖBB) heading

east and north of Vienna (typically to Hungary and the Slovak and the Czech republics) depart from the Südbahnhof, but some also from the Westbahnhof. A few trains to the Czech Republic leave from the Franz-Josefs-Bahnhof. Check your departure station carefully. The Westbahnhof will be downgraded to a national railway station when the new the Südbahnhof is upgraded to Hauptbahnhof (Main Station) in 2012. During the reorganization all trains coming from the south will terminate at Wien Meidling (S-Bahn, U6, Tram 62). For train information and bookings view www.oebb.at or ☎ 05-717 (24 hours).

ARRIVING BY CAR

Vienna is reached from Germany, Salzburg and Linz via the West Autobahn (A1); from the Italian and Slovenian borders and Graz it is reached via the South Autobahn (A2); from the Hungarian and Slovak Borders it is reached via the East Autobahn (A4); and from the Czech border it is reached from Prague via the North Autobahn (A22) and from Brno via the future A5. Currently there are motorway tolls (for which you can buy a *Mautpickerl*—windscreen sticker—at the border) all over Austria; also in neighbouring countries with the exception of Germany, where one is planned.

ARRIVING BY BUS

International bus lines (www.eurolines.at) arrive at the new bus terminal at Erdbergstrasse 200A opposite U3 Erdberg (☎ 798 29 00) or at Arsenalstrasse beside the Südbahnhof (☎ 796 85 52). The S-Bahn leaves from here, together with trams D, O, 18.

ARRIVING BY BOAT

June to September, weekly cruise ships run on the Danube between Passau (Germany) and Vienna. Mid-April to October, there is a daily hydrofoil connection to Budapest. Ships dock at the DDSG (www.ddsg-blue-danube.at) berth near the Reichsbrücke.

NEED TO KNOW GETTING THERE

Getting Around

Vienna is covered in an overlapping network of U-Bahnen (underground trains), Strassenbahnen (trams) and buses. Newsagents (*Tabaktrafik*) sell tickets for public transport. Main U-Bahn and S-Bahn (rapid-transit railway) stations have ticket counters and all of them have ticket machines. Taxis are usually white and can be hired at taxi stands in the city and at the larger public transport terminals. Officially it is not permitted to hail them in the street, but some will stop for you.

INTEGRATED SYSTEM

● Maps and information about the transport network can be obtained at the Wiener Linien information office at the Karlsplatz end of Opern Passage ☎ 790 91 00 and 0810/22 2324.

● Buy tickets for the U-Bahn, Strassenbahn, buses or S-Bahn from newsagents or at the counters in main U-Bahn and S-Bahn stations. An easy one to find is at the Karlsplatz end of the Opern Passage, at the entrance to U1, U2, U4.

● A single journey card must be validated at the entrance to the underground, or on a tram or bus, using the stamping machines. It can be used for one unbroken ride, including changes of line, or changes from S-Bahn/U-Bahn, to tram, to bus. Valid one hour from stamping.

● Penalties for riding without a valid ticket are heavy and checks quite frequent.

TYPES OF TICKET

● Excursion or season tickets are valid on all parts of the network and even on suburban buses (up to the city boundary).

● Individual tickets are much more expensive per ride, and the machines dispensing them on trams are complicated.

● Good-value monthly or weekly tickets allow unlimited travel all over the network for their duration. No photo is required.

● *8 Tage-Karte* (8 strips), each valid for travel all over the network the day it is validated until

TAXIS

● Cabs are efficient and not unreasonably expensive by Austrian standards.

● You can order a cab by phone ☎ 31 300 (airport taxi), 40 100 or 601 60

● Tips are 10 per cent.

● There are supplements for late-night or weekend rides, plus per head and per piece of luggage.

● Taxis ordered by telephone usually arrive in about five minutes in the heart of the city and inner suburbs.

STUDENT VISITORS

● There are nine youth hostels. You need an International Youth Hostel Federation membership card, obtainable on the spot.

● Österreichischer Jugendherbergsverband (Austrian Youth Hostel Association) ✉ Schottering 28 ☎ 533 53 53; www.oejhv.or.at

● From 1 July to 30 September, student hostels in the city become Saison Hotels: information from Academia Hotels (www.academia-hotels.co.at) ✉ Pfeilgasse 3A, A-1080 ☎ 401 76 55. There are rooms for students at the Kolping Movement Centre: Kolpingfamilie ✉ Bendlgasse 10–12 ☎ 813 54 87

1am the following day. If there are two or more of you, validate one strip per person. Start with strip No. 1.

● You can buy blocks of tickets for single rides, as well as 24-hour and 72-hour time tickets (useful for short-term visitors).

● Time tickets and the *8 Tage-Karte* must be validated once at the commencement of the period of use and are then good for the period stipulated.

● *Wien-Karte* is a 72-hour card with discounts on entry charges to many sights.

U-BAHN

● There are five lines. Oddly there is U1, U2, U3, U4 and U6 but no U5. U2 follows a semi-circular route around the Ringstrasse and is now being extended at each end.

● The U-Bahn maps found on platforms are colour-coded and also show connections to other forms of transport. Be careful to note the end-stop of the direction you want; this will be shown on the illuminated sign of the appropriate platform.

● Three lines (U1, U2, U4) meet at Karlsplatz/ Oper.

● Main stations have lifts and/or escalators.

● You may take bicycles into designated cars (except during rush hour).

● The S-Bahn (*Schnellbahn*) is a rapid-transit railway bringing commuters from the suburbs to the major traffic connections of the city.

TRAMS/BUSES

● The route is clearly marked at the tram stop and on a card inside. Check you are going in the right direction.

● Bus routes fill the gaps between the mostly radial tram lines. Night buses on main routes run every 30 minutes from Schwedenplatz after 12.30am until around 5am. No supplement is payable.

● The small hopper buses (1A, 2A and 3A) have circular routes through the Inner City with stops at or near virtually all places of interest.

SENSIBLE PRECAUTIONS

● Lock valuables in your hotel safe and don't carry large amounts of cash. Crime is low in Vienna, but high-season pickpockets are busy.

● Avoid the main railway stations at night and the red-light district along the Gürtel.

LOST PROPERTY

● Report loss or theft to the nearest police station.

● Lost Property Bureau
✉ Wasagasse 22 ☎ 313 44-9211 🕐 Mon–Fri 8–noon

● Railway Lost Property:
☎ 930 00-35656 or 930 00-22222

● Vienna Transport System Lost Property ☎ 790 943-500

DRIVING

● Avoid taking your car into the districts inside the Gürtel and especially into the old city inside the Ringstrasse, where underground parking is expensive and above-ground parking difficult and complicated.

WWW.CITYBIKEWIEN.AT

● At dozens of self-service stations you may hire a bike with a City Bike Tourist Card at a very low rate (have coins prepared) for one calendar day and return it at any vacant bikebox.

Essential Facts

EMBASSIES AND CONSULATES

- **Australia**
  ✉ Mattiellistrasse 2–4
  ☎ 506 74
- **Canada** ✉ Laurenzerberg
  2 ☎ 5313 830 00
- **Ireland** ✉ Rotenturmstrasse 16–18 ☎ 715 4246
- **New Zealand**
  ✉ Argentinierstrabe 20A
  ☎ 318 8505 (consulate
  general)
- **UK** ✉ Jaurésgasse 10
  ☎ 7161 35151
- **US** ✉ Boltzmanngasse 16
  ☎ 313 39 (embassy) or
  ✉ Gartenbaupromenade 2
  (next to Marriott Hotel)
  ☎ 31 339-3005 (consulate)

MONEY

The euro (€) is the official
currency of Austria. Notes
in denominations of 5, 10,
20, 50, 100, 200 and 500
euros, and coins of 1, 2, 5,
10, 20 and 50 cents.

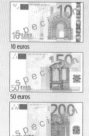

10 euros

50 euros

200 euros

500 euros

ELECTRICITY

- The voltage is 220V AC and two-pin plugs are used.

ETIQUETTE

- Titles are important; if you know which one to use (eg *Herr Doktor*), use it. Address the waiter as Herr Ober, the waitress as Fräulein.

MONEY MATTERS

- Credit cards are accepted by most hotels, leading shops and more expensive restaurants.
- Bankomat machines giving cash against international credit or debit cards with PIN numbers are plentiful in the city.

NATIONAL HOLIDAYS

- 1 Jan
- 6 Jan (Epiphany)
- Easter Monday
- 1 May (State Holiday)
- *Christi Himmelfahrt* (Ascension Day)
- Whit Monday
- Corpus Christi (second Thu after Whitsun)
- 15 Aug (Assumption of the Virgin)
- 26 Oct (National Day)
- 1 Nov (All Saints)
- 8 Dec (Conception)
- 24–26 Dec (everything closes from midday on Christmas Eve)

OPENING HOURS

- Shops: Mon–Fri 9–6, Sat 9–5 (food shops may open earlier). Retailers have the option of Saturday opening, but outside the main shopping areas, some remain closed from noon. Most shops open 9–6 on the four Saturdays before Christmas.
- Banks: Mon–Fri 8–12.30, 1.30–3; Thu 1.30–5.30. In the city some stay open at lunch.
- Offices: Mon–Fri 8–4, but may close earlier on Friday.

PLACES OF WORSHIP

● The Tourismus Pastoral office issues a booklet with details of services for all Christian denominations and Judaism, and where confession in foreign languages may be made ⊠ Stephansplatz 6, 6th floor room 670 ☎ 515 52-335; www.virc.at

● Anglican: Christ Church ⊠ Jaurésgasse 17–19 ☎ 714 8900

● Muslim: Islamic Community of Faith ⊠ Bernardgasse 5 ☎ 526 3122

● Jewish: City Synagogue ⊠ Seitenstettengasse 4 ☎ 532 1884

● Vienna Community Church ⊠ Reformiente Stadtkirche, Dorotheergasse 16 ☎ 505 5233

● Methodist: ⊠ Sechshauser Strasse 56 ☎ 895 8175

● Catholic (Vienna's English-speaking Catholic community): Votivkirche ⊠ Rooseveltplatz 8 ☎ 402 18 30

POST OFFICES

● ⊠ Fleischmarkt 19 ☎ 0577 677-1010 🕔 Daily 6am–10pm

● ⊠ Südbahnhof ☎ 0577 677-71103 🕔 Mon–Fri 7am–8pm, Sat–Sun, hols 9–2

● ⊠ Westbahnhof ☎ 0577 677-1150 🕔 Mon–Fri 7am–10pm, Sat–Sun, hols 9am–8pm

TELEPHONES

● Telephone cards are sold in *Tabaktrafik* shops (newsagents) and at post offices. Some telephones in the Kohlmarkt/Graben area take credit cards.

● To call Vienna from the UK dial 00431. To call the UK from Vienna, dial 0044.

● To call Vienna from the US dial 00431. To call the US from Vienna, dial 001.

● Directory assistance: Austria and the EU ☎ 118 877, everywhere else ☎ 0900 11 8877.

MEDICAL TREATMENT

Medical treatment

● Vienna General Hospital (Allgemeines Krankenhaus) ⊠ Währinger Gürtel 18–20 ☎ 40 400-1964

● The Barmherzige Brüder (Brothers of Mercy) treat patients for free at their hospital ⊠ Mohrengasse 9 (2nd District) ☎ 211 21-0

Medicines

● Pharmacies are normally open Mon–Fri 8–12, 2–6, Sat 8–12.

● English-speaking pharmacists: Internationale Apotheke ⊠ Kärntner Ring 17 ☎ 512 28 25; Schweden-Apotheke, Pharmacie Internationale, ⊠ Schwedenplatz 2 ☎ 533 2911

NEED TO KNOW ESSENTIAL FACTS

Limerick County Library

Language

The Austrian variant of *Hochdeutsch* (High German) is marked enough to warrant a small dictionary for German visitors, but will not trouble the foreign tourist who has learned German. *Wienerisch* (the local dialect of the Viennese) is more difficult, but most natives will respond with the *Hochdeutsch* they have learned in school if addressed in this way by a foreigner.

BASICS	
ja	yes
nein	no
bitte	please
danke	thank you
bitte schön	you're welcome
Grüss Gott	hello
guten Morgen	good morning
guten Abend	good evening
gute Nacht	good night
auf Wiedersehen	goodbye
Entschuldigen Sie bitte	Excuse me please
Sprechen Sie Englisch?	Do you speak English?
ich verstehe nicht	I don't understand
Wiederholen Sie das, bitte	Please repeat that
Sprechen Sie langsamer bitte	Please speak more slowly
heute	today
gestern	yesterday
morgen	tomorrow
jetzt	now
gut	good
Ich heisse...	My name is...
Wie heissen Sie?	What's your name?
Ich komme aus...	I'm from...
Wie geht es Ihnen?	How are you?
Sehr gut, danke	Fine, thank you
Wie spät ist es?	What is the time?
wo	where
wann	when
warum	why
wer	who

USEFUL WORDS	
klein/gross	small/large
kalt/warm	cold/warm
rechts/links	right/left
geradeaus	straight ahead
nahe/weit	near/far
geschlossen	closed
offen	open

OUT AND ABOUT

Wieviel kostet es?	How much does it cost?
teuer	expensive
billig	inexpensive
Wo sind die Toiletten?	Where are the toilets?
Wo ist die Bank?	Where's the bank?
der Bahnhof	station
der Flughafen	airport
das Postamt	post office
die Apotheke	chemist
die Polizei	police
das Krankenhaus	hospital
der Arzt	doctor
Hilfe	help
Haben Sie einen Stadtplan?	Do you have a city map?
Fahren Sie mich bitte zum/zur/nach...	Please take me to...
Ich möchte hier aussteigen	I'd like to get out here
Ich habe mich verlaufen/verfahren	I am lost
Können Sie mir helfen?	Can you help me?

NUMBERS

eins	1
zwei	2
drei	3
vier	4
fünf	5
sechs	6
sieben	7
acht	8
neun	9
zehn	10
elf	11
zwölf	12
dreizehn	13
zwanzig	20
einundzwanzig	21
dreissig	30
vierzig	40
fünfzig	50
sechzig	60
siebzig	70
achtzig	80
neunzig	90
hundert	100
tausend	1000
million	million

AT THE HOTEL/RESTAURANT

die Speisekarte	menu
das Frühstück	breakfast
das Mittagesen	lunch
das Abendessen	dinner
der Weisswein	white wine
der Rotwein	red wine
das Bier	beer
das Brot	bread
die Milch	milk
der Zucker	sugar
das Wasser	water
die Rechnung	bill (check)
das Zimmer	room
Ich bin allergisch gegen...	I am allergic to...
Ich bin Vegetarier	I am a vegetarian

COLOURS

schwarz	black
blau	blue
braun	brown
rot	red
grün	green
weiss	white
gelb	yellow
rosa	pink
orange	orange
grau	grey
lila	purple

Timeline

MUSICAL NOTES

Music has reverberated around Vienna since the days when the *Minnesänger* (poets of chivalry) performed at the Babenberg court in the 13th century. Members of the Habsburg dynasty were patrons of Gluck, Haydn, Mozart and Beethoven, among others.

Key musical dates include:

1782 Mozart's opera *The Abduction from the Seraglio* premieres at the Court Theatre.

1792 Beethoven settles in Vienna.

1828 In June, Franz Schubert completes *Die Winterreise* song cycle. He dies 19 November, age 31.

1867 Johann Strauss Junior's *On the Beautiful Blue Danube* is performed by the Vienna Male Choral Society; it flops.

1897 Gustav Mahler becomes director of the Vienna opera, initiating a period of imaginative productions.

5th–1st century BC The Celtic Boier tribe settles on the site of today's Belvedere Palace.

15 BC The Romans conquer the area.

AD400–791 The Romans withdraw. Charlemagne creates the *Ostmark* (Eastern Region of his empire).

881 The Salzburg annals recall a battle at *Weniam*—the first reference to the name *Wien* (Vienna).

1156 Austria becomes a Babenberg duke-dom and Vienna the ducal residence.

1278 640 years of Habsburg rule begins.

1421 Pogrom against the Viennese Jews. Two hundred are burned alive.

1517 The advent of Lutheranism in Vienna.

1521 The Spanish and German realms of the Habsburgs, ruled by Charles V, are divided. Charles's brother, Ferdinand I, takes Austria.

1529 The first Turkish siege of Vienna.

1551 The Jesuits are invited to the city. The Counter-Reformation begins.

1683 The second Turkish siege attempt.

1805–15 Napoleon's troops twice occupy Vienna. After his defeat, the Congress of Vienna imposes order on Europe.

1848 Revolutions against Habsburg absolutist rule take place. Eighteen-year-old Franz Joseph becomes emperor.

1867 Austro-Hungarian Monarchy is formed.

1916 Franz Joseph dies. The Habsburg Empire is dissolved in 1918.

1922 Vienna becomes one of the Federal States of the Republic of Austria.

1934 Civil War breaks out. Clerico-Fascist dictatorship under Engelbert Dollfuss follows.

1938 Hitler annexes Austria.

1945–55 Vienna is under joint Allied control until the State Treaty restores a free Austrian state.

1995 Austria joins the European Union.

2000 The far right Freedom Party joins the government coalition, amid international controversy.

2007 A new coalition of Social Democrats and Conservatives is formed.

THE RINGSTRASSE

On Christmas Day 1857 Emperor Franz Joseph ordered the demolition of the city bastions and the creation of a great boulevard around the city. The Ringstrasse symbolized an era of wealth, industry and modernization.

THE *ANSCHLUSS*

After the *Anschluss*—the annexation of Austria to Germany by Adolf Hitler—many Viennese went into exile, and artistic and academic talent was lost through Austrian-born Adolf Eichmann's campaign to make Vienna *judenrein* (Jew-free).

Habsburg crown; double-headed eagle; Strauss Monument; Secession's dome of gilded laurel leaves (left to right)

Index

CITYPACK TOP 25
Vienna

WRITTEN BY Louis James
DESIGN CONCEPT Kate Harling
COVER DESIGN AND DESIGN WORK Jacqueline Bailey
INDEXER Marie Lorimer
IMAGE RETOUCHING AND REPRO Michael Moody, Sarah Montgomery
EDITOR Marie-Claire Jefferies
SERIES EDITORS Paul Mitchell, Edith Summerhayes

© AUTOMOBILE ASSOCIATION DEVELOPMENTS LIMITED 2008

First published 1996
Colour separation by Keenes, Andover
Printed and bound by Leo Paper Products, China

A CIP catalogue record for this book is available from the British Library.

ISBN 978-0-7495-5710-2

Published by AA Publishing, a trading name of Automobile Association Developments Limited, whose registered office is Fanum House, Basing View, Basingstoke, Hampshire RG21 4EA. Registered number 1878835.

A03145
Mapping in this title produced from map data supplied by Global Mapping, Brackley, UK. Copyright © Global Mapping/Borch GmbH Publishing
Transport map © Communicarta Ltd, UK

The Automobile Association would like to tha
companies and picture libraries for their assis

Abbreviations for the picture credits are as
(c) centre; (l) left; (r) right; (AA) AA Worl

Front cover AA/M Siebert; **back cover (**
(iv) AA/J Smith; **1** AA/M Siebert; **2-18t (**
4tl AA/J Smith; **5** AA/J Smith; **6cl** © Ös
Österreich Werbung/Trumler; **6cr** AA/J
6bc AA/C Sawyer; **6br** AA/D Noble; **7**
Smith; **7cr** © Österreich Werbung/Ba
© Österreich Werbung/Bartl; **10/11t**
© Österreich Werbung/Bartl; **10/11**
Werbung/Kalmar; **11c** © Österreich
Noble; **13b** © Österreich Werbung
14cbr AA/J Smith; **14br** AA/D Nol
Werbung/Trumler; **16tcr** © Österr
16br Szaszi Hüte; **17tl** AA/J Smit
© Österreich Werbung/Bartl; **17**
Smith; **18tcr** © Österreich Werb
Stockbyte Royalty Free; **19(i)** ©
AA/J Smith; **(iv)** AA/J Smith; **(v**
24tr AA/J Smith; **25tl** © Öster
Smith; **26l** AA/C Sawyer; **26l**
Smith; **27cr** AA/J Smith; **28l**
Werbung/Muhr; **29tr** © Öst
Werbung/Trumler; **30tc** © /
Werbung/Trumler; **31tl** AA
AA/J Smith; **32br** AA/J Sm
Noble; **34br** AA/J Smith;
38-40t © Österreich We
Wiesenhofer; **43-45t** A/
© Österreich Werbung/
Smith; **50tr** AA/J Smith
© Österreich Werbun
53t © Österreich We
AA/J Smith; **54tr** © /
Smith; **56tl** AA/J Sm
57br AA/J Smith; **5**
© Österreich Werb
62-63t AA/C Saw
Werbung/Kalmar
© Österreich We
Smith; **71bl** AA/
Werbung/H Wie
Sawyer; **76** AA
AA/M Siebert;
Smith; **82/83**
84tr AA/J Sm
Smith; **87t** ©
Wiesenhofe
Hedgecoe
Werbung/
Smith; **96**
98l AA/J
Smith; **9**
Smith; '
Werbu
© Öst
108-1
© Ös
114-
AA/
We

Every c...
advance for any
in the following edition c.

CITYPACK TOP 25
Vienna

WRITTEN BY Louis James
DESIGN CONCEPT Kate Harling
COVER DESIGN AND DESIGN WORK Jacqueline Bailey
INDEXER Marie Lorimer
IMAGE RETOUCHING AND REPRO Michael Moody, Sarah Montgomery
EDITOR Marie-Claire Jefferies
SERIES EDITORS Paul Mitchell, Edith Summerhayes

© **AUTOMOBILE ASSOCIATION DEVELOPMENTS LIMITED 2008**

First published 1996
Colour separation by Keenes, Andover
Printed and bound by Leo Paper Products, China

A CIP catalogue record for this book is available from the British Library.

ISBN 978-0-7495-5710-2

Published by AA Publishing, a trading name of Automobile Association Developments Limited, whose registered office is Fanum House, Basing View, Basingstoke, Hampshire RG21 4EA. Registered number 1878835.

A03145
Mapping in this title produced from map data supplied by Global Mapping, Brackley, UK. Copyright © Global Mapping/Borch GmbH Publishing
Transport map © Communicarta Ltd, UK

The Automobile Association would like to thank the following photographers, companies and picture libraries for their assistance in the preparation of this book.

Abbreviations for the picture credits are as follows – (t) top; (b) bottom; (c) centre; (l) left; (r) right; (AA) AA World Travel Library.

Front cover AA/M Siebert; **back cover (i)** AA/J Smith; **(ii)** AA/C Sawyer; **(iii)** AA; **(iv)** AA/J Smith; **1** AA/M Siebert; **2-18t** © Österreich Werbung/ Wiesenhofer; **4tl** AA/J Smith; **5** AA/J Smith; **6cl** © Österreich Werbung/Markowitsch; **6c** © Österreich Werbung/Trumler; **6cr** AA/J Smith; **6bl** © Österreich Werbung/Bartl; **6bc** AA/C Sawyer; **6br** AA/D Noble; **7cl** © Österreich Werbung/Bartl; **7c** AA/J Smith; **7cr** © Österreich Werbung/Bartl; **7bl** AA/J Smith; **7bc** AA/T Harris; **7br** © Österreich Werbung/Bartl; **10/11tc** © Österreich Werbung/Bartl; **10/11cl** © Österreich Werbung/Bartl; **10/11bc** AA/J Smith; **10/11b** © Österreich Werbung/Kalmar; **11c** © Österreich Werbung/Bartl; **13tl** AA/D Noble; **13c** AA/D Noble; **13b** © Österreich Werbung/Kalmar; **14tr** AA/J Smith; **14tcr** AA/J Smith; **14cbr** AA/J Smith; **14br** AA/D Noble; **15b** AA/J Smith; **16tr** © Österreich Werbung/Trumler; **16tcr** © Österreich Werbung/Kalmar; **16bcr** AA/M Siebert; **16br** Szaszi Hüte; **17tl** AA/J Smith; **17tcl** © Österreich Werbung/Kalmar; **17bcl** © Österreich Werbung/Bartl; **17bl** © Österreich Werbung/Popp G; **18tr** AA/J Smith; **18tcr** © Österreich Werbung/Markowitsch; **18bcr** AA/C Sawyer; **18br** Stockbyte Royalty Free; **19(i)** © Österreich Werbung/Lammerhuber; **(ii)** AA; **(iii)** AA/J Smith; **(iv)** AA/J Smith; **(v)** AA/J Smith; **20/21** AA/J Smith; **24tl** AA/J Smith; **24tr** AA/J Smith; **25tl** © Österreich Werbung/Diejun; **25tc** AA/J Smith; **25tr** AA/J Smith; **26l** AA/C Sawyer; **26tr** AA/C Sawyer; **26/27c** AA/J Smith; **27t** AA/J Smith; **27cr** AA/J Smith; **28tl** AA/J Smith; **28tr** AA/J Smith; **29tl** © Österreich Werbung/Muhr; **29tr** © Österreich Werbung/Muhr; **30tl** © Österreich Werbung/Trumler; **30tc** © Österreich Werbung/Trumler; **30tr** © Österreich Werbung/Trumler; **31tl** AA/J Smith; **31tr** AA/J Smith; **32-35t** AA/J Smith; **32bl** AA/J Smith; **32br** AA/J Smith; **33bl** AA/J Smith; **33br** AA/J Smith; **34bl** AA/D Noble; **34br** AA/J Smith; **35b** AA/J Smith; **36t** AA/J Smith; **37** AA/J Smith; **38-40t** © Österreich Werbung/H Wiesenhofer; **41-42t** © Österreich Werbung/ Wiesenhofer; **43-45t** AA/C Sawyer; **46** © Österreich Werbung/Bartl; **47** © Österreich Werbung/Haase; **50tl** © Österreich Werbung/Kalmar; **50tc** AA/J Smith; **50tr** AA/J Smith; **51tl** AA/J Smith; **51tr** AA/J Smith; **52l** AA/J Smith; **52tr** © Österreich Werbung/Trumler; **52/53c** © Österreich Werbung/H Wiesenhofer; **53t** © Österreich Werbung/Bohnacker; **53c** © Österreich Werbung/Kalmar; **54tl** AA/J Smith; **54tr** © Österreich Werbung/Bartl; **55tl** AA/D Noble; **55tr** AA/J Smith; **56tl** AA/J Smith; **56tr** AA/J Smith; **57-58t** AA/J Smith; **57bl** AA/J Smith; **57br** AA/J Smith; **58bl** AA/J Smith; **58br** AA/J Smith; **59t** AA/J Smith; **60t** © Österreich Werbung/H Wiesenhofer; **61t** © Österreich Werbung Wiesenhofer; **62-63t** AA/C Sawyer; **64** AA/J Smith; **65** AA/J Smith; **68tl** © Österreich Werbung/Kalmar; **68tc** AA/J Smith; **68tr** AA/J Smith; **69tl** AA/J Smith; **69tr** © Österreich Werbung/Diejun; **70tl** AA/J Smith; **70tr** AA/C Sawyer; **71t** AA/J Smith; **71bl** AA/M Siebert; **71br** AA/J Smith; **72t** AA/J Smith; **73t** © Österreich Werbung/H Wiesenhofer; **74t** © Österreich Werbung/Wiesenhofer; **75t** AA/C Sawyer; **76** AA/J Smith; **77** AA/J Smith; **80tl** AA/J Smith; **80tr** AA/J Smith; **81tl** AA/M Siebert; **81tc** AA/J Smith; **81tr** AA/J Smith; **82l** AA/J Smith; **82tr** AA/J Smith; **82/83c** AA/J Smith; **83t** AA/J Smith; **83c** AA/J Smith; **84tl** AA/J Smith; **84tr** AA/J Smith; **85t** AA/J Smith; **85b** © Österreich Werbung/Muhr; **86t** AA/J Smith; **87t** © Österreich Werbung/H Wiesenhofer; **88t** © Österreich Werbung/ Wiesenhofer; **89t** AA/C Sawyer; **90** AA/D Noble; **91** © Österreich Werbung/ Hedgecoe (London); **94tl** AA/J Smith; **94tr** AA/J Smith; **95tl** © Österreich Werbung/H Wiesenhofer; **95tr** © Österreich Werbung/Wiesenhofer; **96tl** AA/J Smith; **96tr** © Österreich Werbung/Diejun; **97tl** AA/J Smith; **97tr** AA/M Siebert; **98l** AA/J Smith; **98tr** AA/J Smith; **98cr** AA/J Smith; **99t** AA/J Smith; **99cl** AA/J Smith; **99cr** © Österreich Werbung/Bartl; **100-101t** AA/J Smith; **100b** AA/J Smith; **101b** © Österreich Werbung/Wiesenhofer; **102-104t** © Österreich Werbung/Diejun; **105t** © Österreich Werbung/H Wiesenhofer; **105c** © Österreich Werbung/Wiesenhofer; **106t** AA/C Sawyer; **107** AA/J Smith; **108-112t** AA/C Sawyer; **108tr** AA/J Smith; **108tcr** AA/J Smith; **108cr** © Österreich Werbung/Kalmar; **108br** © Österreich Werbung/Kalmar; **113** AA; **114-125t** AA/J Smith; **120** European Central Bank; **122cr** AA/J Smith; **122br** AA/J Smith; **124bl** © Österreich Werbung/Wiesenhofer; **124br** © Österreich Werbung/Wiesenhofer; **125bl** AA/J Smith; **125br** AA/J Smith

Every effort has been made to trace the copyright holders, and we apologise in advance for any accidental errors. We would be happy to apply the corrections in the following edition of this publication.